GIRL,
Get Your S.W.A.G. Back!
A Soul-Freeing Journey For Women

May the Lord bless you on this journey!

DeYonne Parker

Gem Makers™
Publishing

Girl, Get Your S.W.A.G. Back!
Copyright © 2013 by DeYonne Parker
Published by Gem Makers Publishing
Grayson, GA 30017

Cover Design: Nicole Steele
Cover Art: Dreamstime
Interior illustration: Dreamstime, Shutterstock

ISBN 978-0-9828527-3-6

Printed in the United States of America

ACKNOWLEDGEMENTS

"The Lord is my rock and my fortress and my deliverer, my God, my rock, in whom I take refugee, my shield, and the horn of my salvation, my stronghold". ~ Psalm 18:2

Thank you Heavenly Father. For without **You**, my soul would still be in bondage. I love You and I'm so grateful You have chosen me as a vessel to carry forth Your message to free other souls.

To my loving, wonderful, and burly husband, Will, you are my rock and the protector of all things dear to me. You are, without a doubt, an amazing example for our boys and I consider myself extremely blessed to have you as my partner for life.

To William and Malcolm (my beautiful boys), you are the light of my life. You are the reason I do the things I do. My prayer for you is that you will always put God first in your lives and know WHO you are and WHOSE you are. You were created to be great men and I can't wait to see how you change the world.

To the angel in my life, my Mom, thank you for picking me up when I have fallen, praying for and with me, showing me how to love and be loved, showing me how to give to others and to love people where they are at in their lives. You are my SHERO! I love you.

To my Dad, Jimmy, thank you for being the Father-figure in my life. You have been an amazing pillar of strength for our family and I love you so much.

To my sisters, Lisa and Shonda, words can't express how much I love you. Thank you, Lisa for leading me back to the Father and being an example of the light of Christ. You helped me to remember WHO I was and WHO I belong to and I am forever grateful. Thank you, Shonda for praying for me and with me. Your gift of compassion is incredible and God is going to use your strength and courage to bless others. I'm so lucky to have you both as sisters and friends! God has His hands on both of you.

To my friend, my business partner, and my motivator, Nicole Steele, thank you for encouraging me, praying for me and believing in me enough to give me a platform to showcase my S.W.A.G. You are an AMAZING woman of God.

To my family and my dearest friends (you know who you are), thank you for loving me and praying for me through my trials and my triumphs. You are truly amazing and I love you so very much.

Table of Contents

Foreword

This lady has S.W.A.G.! I know that some of you may be tired of hearing this word in the media and amongst our mainstream youth, but what DeYonne Parker (or Dee as I call her) has done in the creation of this book is REDEFINE the meaning of the word. As you read this book, you will begin to feel as though you know her personally, as if she were your own sister or friend. She invites you into the many facets of her life, "the good, the bad, and the ugly", to assure you that you are not alone in the peaks or the valleys of your life. She reminds us that no matter what our past or even our present looks like, we should be excited and at peace about what God is purposing us to be! But she does make one request – Girl, Get your S.W.A.G. back!

I have the pleasure of knowing this beautiful, strong, and God fearing, woman very intimately. She is my sister. She is my sister biologically and in Christ Jesus. If you're a parent, you may agree that you can see the traits of your children and envision the type of person you believe they will become. Well growing up, we thought we had my sister, Dee pegged. We were raised in the small town (by big city standards) of Omaha,

Nebraska. Yes I said it – Omaha. And I am a witness that BIG things can come out of small packages! We were raised with and around some strong and gutsy women and Dee was one who picked up those genes.

As the baby sister (5 years younger), I always looked up to my two big sisters and they have been such an influence in my life. Watching them grow up let me know what I wanted to do, and what I DIDN'T want to do. I watched them experience great achievements during the highs of their lives, and I watched them in their valleys. It's something when you have front row seats to someone else's life, while not knowing what's really going on behind the curtain.

As Dee discusses in this book, I viewed her as someone who exuded confidence; a confidence that I wanted and tried for many years to mirror. If anyone asked me to describe her, I would say "fiery", "determined", and "CONFIDENT". Anytime I saw her broken, I always saw her pick herself up and dust herself off, showing nothing but courage and resilience in the process.

Because we shared the bond of sisters and best friends, and I thought I knew her well. I mean, from the times she bullied me as a kid, to the times she took me to my first club using her fake ID, I thought I knew her! We were like Frick and Frack; we were inseparable until she moved to Georgia with her husband and the distance challenged our relationship and made it difficult to regularly see each other.

During one of my visits with my sister, we had a true heart-to-heart. You know the long chats you have with your sister or friend until 3am...well, this was one of those times. We sat on her beautiful deck overlooking the lake with candles burning, music playing, and our scarves tied around our heads (got to love your sistas)! I recall listening to her and as she spoke, the Lord let me in on something that I'd been struggling with as I watched her during my visit. He gave me the courage to ask, "Are you really happy?"

I saw her living well with her amazing family, but something was missing. I know my sister well and I could just see something in her eyes. Sometimes we as women try to "put on happy" to either fool others or ourselves without feeling true joy when maybe the cares of this world have stripped it away. True joy is the kind that can only come from the Father Himself. I call it—"God Joy".

When I opened that door of discussion with her, my sister unveiled her biggest secret to me. She had lost her confidence. That "thing" we all saw in her from childhood which separated her from the rest, that fire and zeal that, when written, spelled...D-E-E. I was shocked yet relieved at the same time. That night my sister showed such a vulnerable side of herself that for the first time I felt truly comfortable ministering to her, MY big sister, someone who had always advised me.

It's important that we show our vulnerable sides to the Lord, allowing Him to come in and truly save us. He already knows but He just needs for you to know and to Let Go. *"For whoever wants to save their life, will lose it, but whoever loses their life for me will find it." Matthew 16:25*

My sisters and I grew up knowing the Lord, but now we are walking WITH Him daily. Since that heart-to-heart conversation, every time she and I spoke was like watching the scales fall from the Apostle Paul's eyes. Granted, she wasn't living a life like Paul before his conversion; however, like all of us who know the love of God, she was basking in His glory and experiencing a new depth in Him. Everything she had lost was being restored and she was delivered from everything she no longer needed. As someone once told me, watching her transformation was lovely. The Lord was giving her - her S.W.A.G. back!

DeYonne (Dee) Parker is a natural encourager and promoter of good. Her ability to empower women of all ages and her passion for encouraging them to reach their full potential is something she was created to do. After reading this book, I know that someone's life will be changed and that someone will find strength through Dee's courageous and heartfelt testimonies and, when it's all said and done, I am confident that you are that someone and you will have your S.W.A.G. back!

Evangelist FaLisa Jones
True Foundation

Chapter 1
Broken

At the age of 18, I was a victim of domestic violence and it has taken me a long time to say that out loud. While I wasn't in a relationship with the abuser and wasn't being physically abused, I suffered a terrible injury at his hands, causing my life to take a drastically different direction than I intended.

I had just completed my first semester at the University of Nebraska in Lincoln and I was so excited to be heading home, but a little sad to see my friends head off to different locations. Some were going on exciting vacations with their families and some were headed for internships promising great paths for their futures.

Well, I was headed back to Omaha, Nebraska. Yep...Omaha! One of my childhood friends and I were making plans to have a pretty great summer, filled with parties and whatever college girls could get into during a summer in Omaha! We knew we weren't in a large city but this city is what we knew and we were going to make the best of it. We were determined to have great stories to share with our college friends when we returned back to school next year.

On the drive back to Omaha, I was thinking about how much I had to share with my friends and family about my experience and my plans for the next year.

A couple of days after we arrived home, my mother explained that my older sister, Shonda, was in a relationship with an abusive man and had finally gained the courage to break things off with him. I could see the sadness and worry in my Mother's eyes as she spoke about this man putting his hands on my sister and it broke my heart to know that she had been suffering in silence for so long.

Although we fought like cats and dogs, nobody else dared mess with my big sis while I was around. I always thought she was too pretty to fight, so on a few occasions, I made sure to run interference for her.

Can you imagine a little, skinny kid with glasses who couldn't have weighed more than 80 pounds, trying to protect her big sister by loud talking girls who were twice her size? Well, that was me! Thank goodness they never took me up on my trash talking.

As my Mother continued to explain the story to me, I grew more and more distraught. The look on my mother's face as she was telling me all of this, said enough. She wanted so badly to help her get out of this situation and after hearing all of this, I did too. My mind immediately went into protection mode.

After our discussion, my Mother thought it would be helpful if my friend and I went over to my sister's house to support and comfort her through her efforts to break it off with her boyfriend. She didn't have to ask me twice; I was definitely going to be present!

When we got to her house, I noticed my sister had already packed all of her boyfriend's clothes. She was excited to see us and probably a little relieved to have someone there with her. As we sat and waited for him to arrive, I could tell that my sister was extremely nervous. She was trying to hold small talk with us, but I would catch her in somewhat of a daze and gazing off into the distance.

She looked so different to me. The fire she once had in her eyes was replaced by fear and sadness. I knew that look from when we were children about to receive our punishment for some foolish thing we had gotten ourselves into. If I could have read her thoughts they probably would have said that she was scared about the actions she was preparing to take that night.

We were in the middle of a conversation when we heard a key rattling the keyhole of the front door. We all held our breath for a minute. When the door swung open and her boyfriend walked through it, I could feel my sister's whole body tense up.

He looked around the room, saw bags full of his belongings and asked, "What's this all about?" In a hesitant and nervous voice, she told him that he needed to take his belongings and leave. He gave her a very stern look and walked towards the back of the house to gather more of his things. My friend and I began comforting my sister and reassuring her that she was doing the right thing. I could tell from the expression on her face that breaking free from this man was becoming very real for her.

He walked back into the room with a distant look on his face and demanded that my sister take him to a friend's house. I felt my protection sensors going off. Just as she started to speak, I immediately told him that she wasn't going anywhere with him and that he needed to call a taxi. My sister nervously echoed my response. I knew she was afraid at this point, but we were almost sure he wouldn't touch her while we were in the house.

We were wrong! It happened so fast. One minute we were sitting on the couch while she was telling him to take his belongings and leave, then the next minute I was watching him pull a butcher knife from his pants, stab both my friend and my sister and head towards my direction. As he swung the knife in my direction I put my hands out in front of me and closed my eyes so I couldn't see it coming.

The next thing I felt was a burning sensation going through my hand and up my arm. I opened my eyes and saw the knife had gone through my left hand and missed the intended area...my chest! I looked around and discovered that he stabbed my friend in the chest and my sister in the arm. By the grace of God, we were all still alive. But what occurred after that was mental torment.

While waving the butcher knife around, he began to rant and rave and bark out his plans for what he was going to do with us. He proclaimed to be the devil and that we were all sinners and we had to die for our sins, but he didn't know which one of us to kill first. By this time, I had fallen into a corner and was dizzy from losing so much blood. I was paralyzed with fear and could barely move, trying not to make a sound so he wouldn't turn in my direction. My mind was spinning with so many thoughts that I couldn't formulate one to make an exit plan.

What he did next was one of the most traumatizing events of the whole experience. Over what seemed like hours, we were forced to watch and listen to the physical and verbal abuse of my sister. All I could do was close my eyes and pray that God would end this soon.

When I opened my eyes, I saw my sister's body lying on the floor; I thought she was dead. She wasn't moving or making a sound. At that point, I just wanted this man to do what he said he was going to do...kill me. I couldn't take the torment anymore and I felt helpless and weak. But God showed up in that room.

Unbeknownst to me, during his attack on my sister, the abuser placed the knife on top of a cabinet that was next to the corner I was in. I was still in shock and couldn't move, but from the ground, covered with blood and bruises, my sister rose up and tackled her abuser to the floor.

God breathed life into my sister and gave her indescribable strength. She screamed for me to get the knife. At first, I couldn't process what was happening at that moment, until I heard her scream at me again. Her words rang loud in my ear and I was able to recognize her voice. I saw what she had done and I found the strength to rise up and break the grip of the corner that was holding me captive. I grabbed the knife and swung it at the abuser with all the strength I had left. I could see nothing but a red blur that seemed to fill the whole room. Some say that was from anger, fear and shock. But all I knew is that I was fighting for all of our lives.

That night ended with all of us being rushed to the hospital. The abuser stole my sister's car and drove himself to the hospital, where he was later arrested. He was tried, convicted and sent to prison for about 10 years.

Although he was incarcerated and no longer a threat to us, our lives were forever changed. All three of us were emotionally distraught and mentally exhausted. We all stopped talking about that night because it was too painful for everyone. By the grace of God, our physical wounds healed and we eventually went on with our lives, but we all lost something that night.

As for me, I spent years walking around thinking and saying "I'm OK; I'm fine; it didn't happen to me, I wasn't the real victim." That couldn't have been further from the truth; I wasn't "OK". I struggled for many years trying to rebuild myself, but not really fully acknowledging that something did "happen" to me. Something deep inside of me broke that night, but I wanted to distance myself from that terrible incident and all the memories that came with it.

I convinced myself that it was not my story and I wouldn't allow this to define me. But doing this didn't make the effects of the incident immediately disappear. No, the tentacles of this trauma just unexplainably showed up in various areas of my life.

Where I was once confident, fear took over. As time passed and I got older, I saw myself shrink in areas of my life where I would normally have shown up with boldness. I wouldn't speak up or out even when I knew that I could and should, because I was fearful of the reaction I might receive if I revealed my true thoughts and feelings. Disappointment and hurt caused by other people in my life felt larger than life and took a huge toll on me.

I experienced some pretty low points in my life, my father died a gruesome death in prison, my marriage began to experience serious turbulence and I made some poor choices in trying to cover all the pain I was experiencing. Instead of dealing with all of this, I filed it away with all the other pain. I felt dead inside and convinced myself that I could live this way, but it became evident that I could not.

I remember isolating myself from my family and friends when I was experiencing trials in my life. I didn't want them to see what I was going through because I had always been thought of as the strong, independent, courageous survivor. I thought, "There is no way I can let them see me like this." I didn't want to worry my mother. I felt she had enough to worry about without me adding more on her plate, so I continued living this way for many years.

It felt like my world was crumbling right in front of me and I finally recognized that trying to rebuild myself, **by myself**, wasn't working. I knew God, but I didn't consistently stay in relationship with Him. At the time I didn't know where to begin so I tried desperately to patch the pain with everything but God. But when the temporary fixes stopped working, I knew I had to find Him or I would be lost in a sea of my sorrows. I began seeking God and asking Him to restore in me what He originally created in me. I sought out individuals in my life who I considered to be "safe" to share my story and to gain perspective. It didn't happen overnight, but I did the work it took to feel whole again!

After much prayer and introspection; I was able to get back what I should never have let go – my **S.W.A.G.** Through my relationship with the Father, I found me again and wow, what a wonderful reunion! My soul has never felt freer than it does now. God restored me to what He needed me to be and He placed in me a new mindset and a whole new walk. I found my voice and I'm able to fully use it. It's amazing what God will do in your life when you are fully ready to let go of the past!

Whatever your story and whatever you are currently experiencing, remember that God did NOT design you to be a prisoner of fear. He did NOT place inside of you feelings of unworthiness and doubt. He designed you to be unique, bold, and confident enough to be obedient to His will for your life.

SO, WHY DID I WRITE THIS BOOK?

Well, that's a very good question and there are actually several ways to answer this question. But, let me just give you the skinny version. While in the gym one morning *(trying to keep this over 40 body in shape)*, I was talking to God and asking Him what His purpose was for my life. I was searching for what He required of me.

To my surprise, I heard Him tell me to write a book. At first, I thought, "What? Me – write a book?" "What do I have to write about?" After I calmed down, God began to remind me that He had already placed His messages inside me and that I needed to get myself together and get them out!

I took some time to sit with God to really hear His voice and He began showing me all the places in my life where He turned my messes into messages. He showed me the countless times that He had broken the chains of bondage in my life and allowed me to walk confidently and boldly in my destiny. I started to get extremely excited about the thought of being used to help others reach the soul-freeing joy that I feel in my life right now. I began to embrace the idea of God using me to help others break free from the bondage, bitterness and brokenness that might be preventing them from living full, rich lives. So, why did I write this book? I wrote it for YOU.

GETTING THE MOST OUT OF THIS BOOK

You're probably wondering what you can expect from a book like this and asking, "Is it a self-help book?" **Yes.** Is it an inspirational book? **Yes.** Is it a workbook? ***Absolutely!*** It's all those things and more. It was written to help you help yourself break barriers that you've been avoiding until now. My prayer is that it will inspire you to begin being an active participant in your life again. But, having said that, you'll need to do the WORK required in this book to push you out of the somewhat comfortable stage you're in and into the next level of your life.

You had to know with a title like **"Girl, Get Your S.W.A.G. Back!"** that you were going to be in for a different kind of experience. Well, you are correct, my friend. So, get a pen or pencil (and maybe a box of tissues) because during the course of your reading you'll be asked to answer thought-provoking questions, recall specific situations in your life and write meaningful action steps for creating a plan to get your S.W.A.G. back.

As you read through each chapter, I challenge you to let your thoughts be transformed and your concerns and cares be removed. Ponder and meditate on the **Soul-Spirations** - inspirational messages designed to inspire and uplift your soul. Thoughtfully and *honestly* answer the **Soul-Freeing Questions** found after each chapter.

Throughout the book, I hope you're able to see a piece of yourself somewhere in my testimony. I hope you're challenged enough by the soul-freeing questions to write your truth and provoked enough to take the necessary actions to start changing it. By the end of this book, it's my desire that you're inspired and motivated to allow God to break the chains that are restricting you from moving forward.

FIND A S.W.A.G. PARTNER

There may be times when you feel like this journey is too overwhelming and you aren't reaping the benefits. There were so many times that I started down this path and stopped because I wasn't seeing the results fast enough. But I had an incredible support system that encouraged me along the way. You may experience some emotional ups and downs, but don't give up!

As you take this journey, it's extremely important that you find someone you trust that will encourage you during the times when you feel the most challenged. Tell them what you're doing and ask them to read the book with you. At the very least, have them act as your accountability partner to help you stay the course. Having a support system around you is such a valuable piece to all of this. You'll be surprised how they'll show up in your life when you need them the most.

YOUR COMMITMENT

Have you ever looked at the definition of the word "commitment"? According to the Merriam-Webster Dictionary, it means *"an agreement or pledge to do something in the future"*. In order to complete this journey, you have to make a commitment a, pledge for your future, to fully go through the process. We make promises and commitments to people all the time, but when will you make one to yourself? Why not start today?

By writing a commitment letter to yourself, you're committing to doing whatever it takes to re-claim the life that God uniquely created for you. You're also making a promise to find yourself again and to show up strong, confident and bold in your life.

Use the space on the following page (or in your S.W.A.G. Journal) to write your Commitment Letter. It should include what you want to get from this experience, what you're willing to commit to in order to get it and what actions you will take to maintain your outcome. Remember, this letter is from <u>YOU</u>, to <u>YOU</u> and for <u>YOU</u>. Take your time and really give some thought to what you want. This is your chance to say exactly what you want to yourself and pour out your heart's desires.

Your Commitment Letter

*Dear*_____,

(Write Your Name)

_____

_____

_____

_____

_____

_____

_____

_____

_____

_____

_____

_____

_____

Love,

_____

(Write Your Name)

Chapter 2
What Is S.W.A.G.?
And How The Heck Do I Get It Back?

"**W**here did it go; the stuff that made me who I am?" "I used to be confident and full of joy. What happened to me?" Does this sound like a familiar conversation that you have had with yourself? Well, this is what would constantly play in my head during certain seasons in my life.

I would sit and think about it but never knew exactly what was going on or what I could do about it. If this sounds like a conversation you've had with yourself or questions you've asked yourself, then *girl*, somewhere along life's winding road, you lost your S.W.A.G.!

Now, I know what you're thinking; but no, I'm not referring to the dictionary's definition of "swag – *loot, free gifts or prizes*" and "No", I'm not necessarily talking about the slang definition of "swag – *coolness, style, sway in your walk*"; although that does have a little something to do with it. So, what am I talking about and how do you get it back?

Allow me to break it down for you. For the purposes of this book, S.W.A.G. stands for:

S   **Self-Confidence** – Regain your confidence and discover your true worth and value. Understand WHO and WHOSE you are.

W   **Walk with God** – Restore, refresh and rekindle your relationship with God and allow Him to order your steps.

A   **Attitude of Gratitude** – Adjust your attitude. It will take you to great heights and being grateful will help keep you there.

G   **God-given Gifts and Talents** - Get off your gifts and talents and use them to change the world!

REALITY CHECK

Ok, so now that you know what S.W.A.G. is, how did you lose it and how do you go about getting it back? We will get to all of that real soon, but first, let's start with a reality check!

Many of us have experienced trials and tribulations in our lives that have knocked us off our "A" game and maybe even had us "down and out" for quite a while. I've been through some soul-shaking experiences that had me wondering if I would ever recover. You might be feeling like that right now, but I can tell you that this is only temporary. You didn't get to this place in your life all in one day, so know that rebuilding and restoring your life is not an overnight process; it will take time and effort on your part. What truly matters is that you get back up, dust yourself off and begin again!

While this may be your first step to breaking the chains of bitterness, brokenness and bondage, it's a pretty bold step but one that will truly be rewarding. It may feel a bit uncomfortable at times, but keep going. You may get distracted, but find your focus. It's up to you to change or remove those obstacles in your life that have you living in bondage and despair.

YOUR CHANGE IS NOT FOR EVERYONE

While this soul-freeing journey is a personal one, you are still playing various roles in your life (mother, wife, sister, daughter, friend, etc.), which means that you have other people in your life that will notice changes in you. When you begin to talk, walk and act differently than before, people will notice. And while you may be glowing and beaming with God's light, your family, friends and loved ones may not be quite ready for the brand new you, but it's ok; keep pressing forward! You don't need to seek approval to make positive changes in your life, but be aware that you may not initially receive the accepting responses you desire from everyone in your life.

People experience change in very different ways. Your friends and loved ones may not be expecting this from you because they're used to who you are right now. They need time to process the new changes they see in you and maybe even mourn the loss of the relationship with the old you. Be patient with them; they didn't receive the memo, alert or notice that you were going to make some radical changes in your life that may impact the way you show up in their lives.

Until they can truly see the benefits of the new you, it may feel like something has been taken away from them. The more consistent you are with how you live your new life, the quicker you will see the support from your family and friends return and they will then become your cheering section.

You may also see people struggle with the changes in

you because they feel obligated to change with you. It's almost like your life becomes a reflection of how they're living. You may lose a few people along the way but that's OK, make no apologies. It may be necessary for God to remove people from your life who will hinder you from experiencing all that He has for you. My mother used to always say, "People are meant to be in your life for a reason, season or a lifetime". It may be time to sift through your life and find your lifetime people; you'll need them.

WHERE DID YOU LOSE YOUR S.W.A.G.?

To get your S.W.A.G. back you have to first understand where you lost it! The "who?", "what?", "when?", "where?", "why?", and "how?" matter. Whether you've experienced great tragedy in your life or life's circumstances have caused you to lose your balance, uncovering the details matter. Getting very clear about where you are in your life and what you've come through allows you to avoid repeating what caused you to get here in the first place. It's time to get real with yourself and express what's truly going on. No matter how ugly the truth is or how painful it may feel, you have to uncover it and look at it for what it is. It may bring up some uncomfortable or painful points in your life, but don't let these feelings discourage you. You need to feel them so that you can effectively deal with them.

REFLECT, MOURN, MOVE

The moment you release yourself from the weight of all that you are carrying, you can then begin to move forward. God wants to do something magnificent in your life. But before He can, you have to be willing to give up the pain of past hurts caused by other people. Let go of the bitterness in your heart and free yourself of the bondage that imprisons you. Are you willing to do that? Or do you want to keep holding on to all that heavy baggage?

When I was about 30 years old I made a bold decision to go speak with a therapist about some trials I was experiencing in my marriage. I convinced myself that I was going to go in and be fully transparent about what I was feeling. I thought, "After all, this person doesn't know me and I'll probably never see her again, so, what do I have to lose?"

During the first session the therapist asked me to explain the reason I made the appointment and how I needed help. I began telling her the sorted details of what was occurring in my marriage and how it made me feel. She sat there quietly for a moment and made some notes, but what she did next both surprised and upset me.

She began asking me some pretty tough questions that I wasn't quite prepared to answer. She asked me questions about my childhood, my upbringing, my father and my past relationships. It felt like someone was ripping off bandages from wounds that I had "effectively" covered up for years! I was angry, embarrassed, and uncomfortable. I wanted to immediately leave her office so, I DID! Yep, I marched right out of her office and told her that I was "fine" now and I would no longer need her services.

I thought to myself, "Who is she to be asking me questions like that? The truth was, I wanted her to validate my feelings about my husband at that time and to tell me what I wanted to hear...that I was right and he was wrong! I was not expecting her to turn the tables and start talking about me. *Oh no!* This was not about me, or so I thought! I later realized, when I went back to see her (yes, I went back!), that she was making me deal with areas of my life that I didn't think were relevant to my situation. I didn't think it mattered because that was the past, but, it did matter.

All the experiences in our life shape and mold us in some way. Each one is like a layer wrapped around our hearts and our souls. It's almost like peeling off the layers of an onion. Once I was able to freely talk about my past experiences to someone I deemed "safe", I could feel the layers begin to fall away. What layers are you ready to shed?

MOVING FORWARD

I'm sure the experiences in your past and those you are going through right now are very real to you. They may seem very heavy and daunting, but you have to move forward. It's time! Are you ready to give up all the stuff that's holding you back from living free? Are you ready to fight for the life you were created to live? Great, because God wants more for and from you and He thinks you are worth the fight! It's time you think the same about yourself.

The following chapters will go deeper into each area of the acronym S.W.A.G. You will be encouraged to examine where you are currently in that area and further identify where you want to be. As you read this book, take this time to be honest and be willing to look at things from a different perspective. Now, take a minute to close your eyes...take a deep breath and ask God to give you the strength you'll need to remain focused and the courage you'll need to finish the journey.

Now, find a quiet place or a space where you can think and answer the following soul-freeing questions. The purpose of having you write the answers to these questions is to help you express yourself in ways that you might not feel comfortable doing verbally. You can later revisit them and reflect back on what God brought you through. If you need more space, grab your S.W.A.G. Journal or a notebook to capture your answers, thoughts and "Aha" moments.

Ok, one last thing before you begin this life changing journey. Using whatever social media site you choose or texting device you use, inform your friends or family members that you are on a journey to get your S.W.A.G. back. You can simply say "On my way to getting my S.W.A.G. back!" or #SWAGBOUND. Be bold and creative!

Informing your friends and family will not only help build your support system, but it will make this a very real experience for you.

Now, ready...set...GO...GET YOUR S.W.A.G. BACK!

oul-Spiration

"Take back the life you were created to live and shed those past hurts; God wants to replace it with joy!"

Soul-Freeing Questions

1. When it comes to your S.W.A.G. , which S.W.A.G. area do you feel you need to focus on the most and why?

    _____

    _____

    _____

2. If you could draw or describe a picture of your CURRENT life, what would it look like?

    _____

    _____

    _____

3. If you could draw or describe a picture of your DESIRED life, what would it look like?

    _____

    _____

    _____

4. What past experiences have you allowed to prevent you from living up to your fullest potential?

    _____

    _____

    _____

5. What changes are you committed to making to live your DESIRED life?

_____

_____

_____

6. What barriers do you need to be mindful of that may prevent you from living your DESIRED life? How will you overcome these barriers?

_____

_____

_____

_____

_____

_____

_____

 Be encouraged by Matthew 11:28

Chapter 3
Self-Confidence

It's what gives you that sway in your walk, that pep in your step and that lift in your voice that commands respect and attention. Because of *it,* people will flock to you like bees flock to honey. *It* can be the first thing people see when you walk through the door and the last thing they remember as you make your bold exit! But on the other hand, *it* is often misused, misunderstood, and totally taken for granted.

We lose *it* when we allow fear or doubt to reign in our lives. We quickly and unknowingly give *it* away without fully understanding and evaluating the real value of *its* true worth.

What could be so powerful that *it* could cause people to stop in their tracks or turn their heads to get a second look, but yet be so vulnerable that we can lose *it* at the first sign of tribulation? Your **self-confidence!**

THE POWER OF SELF-CONFIDENCE

There's nothing quite as magnetic as being in the presence of someone who knows their worth and is confident in their abilities. It's downright infectious and invigorating. Am I right? You take note of someone who commands the room when they walk in and you practically hang on every word as if it they were speaking a language that you've just heard for the first time. You can't quite figure out why they are so interesting or why you want to constantly be in their presence, but you are secretly hoping that just a sprinkle of their magical sparkle will somehow fall onto you. This is the power of **self-confidence**!

After reading this description, you might've been able to identify with this person or you might've been that person not too long ago, but are currently lacking in the self-confidence department these days. Whatever the case may be, we can all recognize confidence when we see it.

I'm sure if you were asked to define self-confidence you'd be able to rattle off a few quick definitions. But for the sake of this book, let's humor ourselves by taking a closer look at how the Merriam-Webster

Dictionary defines self-confidence:

Self-confidence <self-con-fi-dence>
1 a: *a feeling or consciousness of one's*
powers or of reliance on one's circumstances

The first part of this word is "self"; that means you. This means your self-confidence starts with **YOU.** You OWN it. Nobody else can get it for you or take it from you unless you give them permission to do so. You own how you feel and what you think about yourself and your abilities.

In addition to Merriam-Webster's definition, I'd add that self-confidence is an incredible gift from God that comes from the inside out and assures you that you can do anything through Him and with His grace. So, when we have self-confidence, I mean when we *truly* have it; you know WHO you are and WHOSE you are and nothing or no one can stop you from accomplishing what you set out to do.

The unfortunate truth of the matter is that some of us trade our self-confidence in for what others think and feel about us. We begin to give weight to words that have the ability to penetrate the armor of our spirit by believing the ugliness of what the world has to say about us. And just like that, we find ourselves in a dark place of self-doubt.

THE WEIGHT OF SELF-DOUBT

Self-doubt is exhausting, emotionally, mentally and physically. But what's even more exhausting, is the charade that we put on for others so they won't really see what's going on "behind the curtain". The work that it takes to appear like we're "fine" and confident when we know we're really shrinking inside, can seriously wear us out. This became evident during a particular season in my life.

I was having one of my many "Sissy" chats with my youngest sister, Lisa (who is also my wonder twin and S.W.A.G. partner!), and I was excitedly sharing with her that I was invited to speak at a women's brunch alongside some pretty powerful speakers. I explained that while I was excited and honored, I doubted my ability to stand and deliver a quality presentation. I didn't feel like I measured up to these powerful women and I didn't want to make a fool of myself.

After hearing my concerns, my sister said something that made me pause for a moment. She told me that she had always looked at me as the confident one in our family and that she truly admired that about me (I was almost brought to tears. Ok, I cried...LOL!). She explained that she watched me stand up for justice during unjust situations at my high school. She went on to say that, in my younger years, it was my confidence that showed up on the track field every time I took position at the starting line of a race.

I was flattered that my sister thought so highly of me, but I was also heavy hearted because I was carrying around a deep-seated secret. I knew it was time to let her in on it. I began to explain that the confidence she once saw in me had been replaced with fear and self-doubt. I explained that several turbulent experiences in my life and marriage had shaken my confidence and nearly destroyed it.

My sister was completely surprised by my confession and began to inquire about what happened to me that made me lose that strong confident presence she admired. Up until this point, I'd been successful at hiding my lack of confidence and covering up all the scars from the pain I was carrying around. But my facade had come to an end. Exposing my big secret to my sister was like having a big weight lifted from my shoulders.

I had to ask myself, "Who am I doing this for?" and "Why?". Through all of my charades, what was I gaining? Clearly, I wasn't doing it for me because I was miserable and exhausted. No, I did it to make other people in my life comfortable with what they had always expected from me...a confident, survivor. If you're suffering from a lack of self-confidence and starring in a master illusion charade, it's time for you to ask yourself the same question...Why"?

AN "AHA" MOMENT

A few years ago I read *The Confident Woman* by Joyce Meyer; a great read that provides really insightful points. One statement really hit home and was like an "aha" moment for me. It read:

> *"Fear is a dangerous virus, because a fearful person has no confidence and can never reach her potential in life. She won't step out of her comfort zone to do anything – especially*

something new or different. Fear is a cruel ruler and its subjects live in constant torment."

Wow! This statement is so powerful and really speaks to the main reason we hold ourselves hostage and give away our self-confidence. It's this type of fear and lack of trust in our God-given capabilities that stops us from completing and carrying out God's purpose for our lives.

Think about that for just a second...fear can hold you back from being all that God created you to be. I was carrying all this weight around because I thought I had lost *"my"* confidence, when in actuality I had lost my confidence in the Lord. Our confidence comes from trusting and believing who God says we are in His eyes. That's powerful!

The moment I re-discovered that it was God who gave me confidence and that through Him I could do ALL things (Philippians 4:13), my thoughts were forever changed and the weight began to lift. I realized that God didn't want me walking around in a constant state of fear and torment. That state of mind goes against everything He designed us to be. He wants us to be strong and courageous and He promises to be with us wherever we go (Joshua 1:9).

It took a few more bumps and bruises to my soul, for me to really figure this out and believe it. But, this meant that I could finally **LET GO** of the fear I had embedded in my spirit because I have been fearfully and wonderfully made by the Father (2 Timothy 1:7). I'm not trying to over simplify this process because I know what it feels like to be a prisoner to fear and to lose the confidence I once had in my life. But you can be set free, if you totally surrender all your fears, burdens, worries and anxieties to Him.

THE FREEDOM OF SELF-WORTH

How much are you worth? Your true worth and value starts with you knowing the answer to this question. Once you know **WHO** you are and **WHOSE** you are, you'll begin to take the limits off your abilities. You'll do things that you never thought you could do. You'll go places you never thought you'd be able to go and you'll say things you never thought you could say. The feeling is absolutely incredible and is far greater than carrying around the weight of self-doubt.

I had the opportunity to attend a powerful women's

conference that focused on fully jumping into your purpose. Initially, I wasn't quite sure what to expect from this conference, but I was open to receive what I was supposed to get. The morning kicked off with a session on interviewing skills. Well, I had no choice but to attend this session, since all the other sessions were full. I thought to myself, "I guess I could always brush up on my interviewing skills!".

I took my seat and waited to hear the usual interviewing skills spiel from the speaker. But, I was pleasantly surprised when I heard one of the speakers drop a golden nugget on us. She talked about how women, during interviews, speak in terms of "we" or "us" instead of "I". We tend to say things like "We accomplished so much in such a short time" as opposed to saying "I was able to complete X, Y, and Z in only 2 weeks."

She went on to say that a lot of women are uncomfortable with talking about themselves and their accomplishments because they don't want to sound boastful. At this point, she had my full attention and I was waiting to hear the next nugget she was going to drop. She ended her spiel by saying that we need to be comfortable and confident when talking about our worth because opportunities will pass us by without us expressing one word about our abilities. Wow...what a powerful nugget of knowledge. I felt like running up and giving the lady a high-five and a fist bump and actually did after the session was over.

I began recalling the countless times that I had given credit away to somebody else for my work. I recalled the times I supported and encouraged others in their accomplishments, but I would fade to black many times when it came to talking about my own. Starting to sound familiar? Where are you fading in your life?

The lack of confidence in your abilities not only impacts your life but it also impacts the lives of those around you. Let me explain. If you're not walking fully in your potential and are fearful to step out into what you are called to do, then you may be holding someone else back from doing what they are called to do. We're all connected in one way or the other. Your confidence may create a platform for someone else to carry out their assignment (we'll discuss the gifts and talents area in greater detail later in the book, keep reading).

The point here is that you have a choice. Either keep your self-confidence shackled in the basement of your soul and never live up to your fullest potential or stop hiding behind fear, doubt and anxiety and embrace the words "I" and "Me". How will you ever know what you're capable of doing if you don't allow yourself to try? We all have a job to do in this world and it can't be done if we're not confident enough to star in our own story. It's time you live to tell your story and to leave imprints on the lives of others.

Here are a few tips to help you come from behind the curtain of self-doubt:

- Find a scripture that speaks to your heart. Read and meditate on it until you believe it.

- Get involved in activities that will push you out of your comfort zone (volunteer, exercise, etc.).

- Change your walk. You are royalty, the daughter of The King. Hold your head up and strut!

- Speak up and out. Let your voice be heard during discussions.

- Don't be afraid to share your opinion when it

adds value to a discussion.

- Practice sharing your accomplishments with a friend. Intentionally express how you contributed or accomplished a task or project.

Soul-Spiration

"Free yourself from the shackles of fear and confidently step out on the platform God gave you."

Soul-Freeing Questions

1. On a scale from 1 – 10 (10 being the highest level). Rate your level of confidence. If you rated yourself lower than a 10, explain why and discuss this with your S.W.A.G. partner.

   _____

   _____

   _____

2. Think about a time when you wish you had been more confident or bold. What held you back?

   _____

   _____

   _____

3. In what areas of your life do you need to be more confident? Why?

   _____

   _____

   _____

4. Write a personal advertisement of yourself. It should include your strengths and goals. Share it with your S.W.A.G. partner.

   _____

   _____

   _____

5. Revisit the rating you gave your level on self-confidence. What actions can you take to get closer to level 10? Complete the following sentences.

In the next 7 days, I will...

_____

_____

_____

In the next 30 days, I will...

_____

_____

_____

In the next 60 days, I will...

_____

_____

_____

 Be encouraged by Hebrews 13:6 and Psalm 139:14

Chapter 4
Walk With God

This chapter was my favorite one to write. I was both excited and anxious to write it because I wanted to ensure that I honored, glorified and represented my Heavenly Father while revealing a lot about my own walk. I'll warn you now, you may want to get a hot cup of tea or coffee, your S.W.A.G. Journal and a box of tissues because we're about to go deep! This is by far the most impactful, imperative and also the longest chapter in the book. This part of your journey is the very crux for getting your S.W.A.G. back!

The current state of your spiritual life will determine how you receive this chapter. But no matter where you're at, hopefully you'll see glimpses of yourself weaved between each word and paragraph. If you don't currently have a relationship with God, my prayer for you is that by the end of this chapter, you'll be encouraged to diligently seek Him and begin building a relationship so that you may come to know His perfect love. You'll experience no other love like it and He'll move your life in directions that you could never imagine!

Having God at the center of your life will not only make the difference in the choices you make and the direction you take in your life, but you will also gain an incredible love that can't come from anyone but the Heavenly Father.

As you read earlier, self-confidence plays a major role in your life and can propel you into the greatest spaces and places. But I firmly believe that your confidence comes from knowing WHO you are and WHOSE you are. When you have a strong relationship with God, you feel deep down in your core that you can do ALL things through Him, but not just "do" them, but do them boldly. Your walk truly does change! You begin to walk taller and strut more confidently. You KNOW that you're a child of the Most High and nothing or nobody can tell you any different! If you don't have that feeling or if you have lost that feeling, this chapter is for you.

WALKING AWAY

Some of us know God very well, but for one reason or another we've broken up with Him, put Him on the shelf and walked away. Your break up with God may be due to painful experiences in your life that caused you to question God's presence or existence during those times. Or you decided to take the reins back from God because you may not be seeing the results you want for your life come to pass quickly enough. Or you might've had some bad experiences with people in the church (who profess to be "Christians") that made you question what having a relationship with the Father is really about. Or you may have abandoned your walk because your family or loved one doesn't share your beliefs and has caused you to doubt them as well. Whatever your reason for breaking up with God or why you've put Him on the shelf and walked away, it's time to dig deep and get real with yourself.

Sure, this might be one of the hardest conversations you may have with yourself, but it's time to put on your "big girl" shoes and get your walk back. You might be thinking that you've gone too long or too far for you to re-kindle or begin a relationship with Him, but that couldn't be further from the truth, my friend!

I know all too well about running from God. I had my running shoes on for a number of years. I took the reins from the Lord and began to run my life in the direction I *thought* it should go.

After crashing and burning a few times, I assumed it

was too late and that I had wrecked my relationship with God. I thought the damage was irreparable and I was just too embarrassed to even start talking to Him again, as if He didn't already know the things I'd done! Girl, this couldn't be further from the truth. If this is at all how you're feeling, stop right now and say these words, out loud with extreme attitude and conviction, "The devil is a liar"! Christ's love for you is so wide, long, high and deep that you couldn't out run it even if you tried (Ephesians 3:18). He wants you to run back to Him so that He can build you back up again.

God made the first move when He gave His son, Jesus Christ, to wipe our slates clean. His Word tells us that we all fall short of His glory and that if we ask for forgiveness and repent, He will forgive us of our sins and remember them no more (2 Corinthians 5:19). When we truly accept Christ as our Lord and Savior and make God the head of our lives, He makes us a new creature, the old has passed away and we are brand new (2 Corinthians 5:17-18). That's a powerful move by the Father and He's waiting for you to make the next one!

TRYING TO FILL GOD'S SHOES

When Malcolm, my youngest son, was about 4 years old he asked, "What size shoe do you think God wears?". I didn't quite know how to answer that question so I said, "They probably have to be some pretty enormous ones to keep up with all of His children." After I tucked little Malcolm in bed that evening, I started to think about the many times I tried to fill God's enormous shoes with things that just didn't fit. And frankly, I think He had quite a laugh at how ridiculous it was for me to even try.

When we don't feel God's presence in our lives it leaves a void or a lack of fulfillment lurking in the depths of our souls. Left unfilled, the yearning seems to grow stronger and the tornado of frustration shows up in ways that will run over anyone in its path. Out of desperation, we try to fill this void with temporary and superficial things that don't last but have the potential to damage us or those around us.

In my experience, I found that the Lord is the Master of filling voids. NOTHING I tried could fill the God-shaped hole in my heart and it wasn't for lack of trying. I remember trying so hard to convince myself that if I just had this one "thing" I would be fulfilled or if I could just go to this one "place" I would be happy or if my marriage was problem-free everything would be perfect. In reality, when I received those things I longed for, I was still left feeling unfulfilled.

Remember the Tin Man from the Wizard of Oz (or my favorite, The Wiz with Michael Jackson) who wanted nothing more than something to be placed inside of him that allowed him to feel. He was determined and convinced that he would receive what he longed for from the great and powerful Wizard of Oz. But as it turned out the Wizard was just a mere man behind a flashy curtain and blowing nothing but smoke. As the story draws to a close, we see a misled Tin Man finally discover (through the encouragement of Dorothy) that what he had exhaustedly searched for was in him the entire time.

Not unlike the Tin Man's quest, some of you are on that same expedition, running down life's Yellow Brick Road, frantically grasping at anything that will fill that gaping God-shaped hole in your heart. You're trying as hard as you can to fill that emptiness with something satisfying and fulfilling. Aren't you tired of feeling like something is missing and exasperated from spending so much time searching for it? You may have found some temporary fillers to soothe the longing and numb the pain for now but how long will that last?

We are directly connected to the Father and created in His likeness. When we put things in our spirit that attempt to replace Him, over time it will be rejected because it just doesn't fit. What you've been searching for is already inside of you and no matter how hard you try, you can't fill God's shoes!

You won't need those artificial fillers when you make God the source of all things in your life. He'll fill you with such a phenomenal power that you won't need anything else to make you feel complete. It's time to come clean and replace the artificial fillers with the love of Christ.

HE WANTS YOUR ATTENTION

When I think about my walk with God, it brings tears to my eyes and takes my breath away and, if I'm really being honest, it also gives me a belly laugh! I was so naïve to think I was running things in my life and that I didn't need to do it God's way!

I mean I just know He was getting a good chuckle watching me walk into walls that He could easily have moved. Thank God for revelation and new beginnings!

Like most of us, I was introduced to God by a parent taking me to church when I was very young. My mother would take me and my sisters to church services on a pretty regular basis when I was in elementary and middle school. When I reached my teenage years, going to church was simply something I had to do to earn the privilege to go roller-skating on Sunday evenings. That was the rule in Carol Jean's house!

When we were in attendance, I listened to the lessons about Jesus and how He died for our sins. I watched church folk feverishly praise and worship the Lord until they were nearly hoarse from singing and shouting so loudly. I watched as the saints shouted and "got happy" from being filled with the Holy Spirit, which both scared and intrigued me at times. I experienced elaborate and lengthy prayer sessions that were filled with eloquent praises to the Almighty. And somewhere between the ages of 10 – 12, I was dunked in a pool of water (with a Jeri Curl cap on my head) and baptized in the name of Jesus. But, even after all of that, I can honestly say that I still didn't understand who God or Jesus really was and why everyone was so excited at the mere mention of their names.

As I got older I prayed and went to church, like I was taught. I was a "church-going Christian" that still didn't quite understand the power of God that everyone talked about. I felt like I was missing out on something truly big and nobody was telling me the secret of how to get it! So, I just went with the flow. I knew of God and Jesus, but it wasn't until I was about the age of 27 that I had a true personal encounter with Him.

In 1999, my husband and I moved from Nebraska to Georgia where we planned to raise our children. I was pregnant with our first son and we were both excited and a little nervous about his arrival. We really didn't know anyone in Georgia, so this was all new territory for both of us and we had to truly rely on one another. To add to the difficulties of adjusting to a new state and all new surroundings, we were also experiencing some issues in our marriage.

This wasn't the first time we had experienced issues in our relationship, but it was the first time that I had no one to run to for support or a shoulder to cry on. I longed for the company of familiar faces, but since all my friends and family were in Nebraska, there was nobody I could call to come over or for me to drop in on them for a visit. I tried making friends on the job where I worked but, I was too pregnant and way too swollen to hang out with any of them. I also lived too far from them to risk taking a leisurely drive which would have probably ended up with me frantically searching for directional signs that may have led me down the wrong path. I was truly all alone, or so I thought.

One evening, I was lying on the couch watching TV, trying to distract myself from all the emotions I was feeling when I felt a warm embrace and heard a voice whisper, "You are not alone". I was too tired to question what I was hearing, but I felt so at peace and so comforted in that moment that I drifted off to sleep. Somehow I knew that was the voice of God and that His loving arms were holding me in my "midnight" hour. I remember feeling safe and surrounded by love. It was one of the most indescribable and beautiful embraces that I had ever felt and I wanted nothing more than to just stay in that moment.

I began to realize that God had purposely placed me in a position with no friends or family in near reach. Instead of seeking Him in my "midnight" moments, I was giving my attention to my emotions and feelings and mourning the absence of friends and family that were always there to lift me up. He wanted my attention and He got it by removing all barriers to Him. He had waited long enough!

In what areas of your life is God trying to get your attention? Who are you putting in place of God's great counsel and wisdom? While people may provide us with immediate responses to our needs and comfort us when we're not at our best, they can never take the place of all that you personally receive from God.

You might be experiencing a rough patch in your life right now and may welcome the opportunity to be distracted. I totally understand that feeling. What I've learned in my walk over the years is that God allows us to go through some impossible trials in our lives, because that's where He does His best work (Psalm 119:71). When we have done all *we* can do, the Lord shows up; right there in the middle of our impossibilities! He'll use whatever He needs to use to get you to turn toward Him. He wants your attention and He will do what it takes to get it.

GROWING PAINS

I was raised by a sassy, strong, single mother who was very independent and wasn't afraid to tell you that you didn't pay the rent at 4512 Spencer Street! My Momma was not the one to be toyed with when it came to her independence and her girls. She taught us to be just as strong, independent and tough-minded. She raised us to the best of her ability and poured every ounce of herself into us. She wanted us to understand our value and to command the respect she felt we deserved in this world.

I learned how to carry myself as a young woman and not to be taken for granted by anybody. I was determined not to let "any man walk all over me" or tell me what I "should" or "shouldn't be doing." I took my mother's word as law and I had the strong woman's mantra down to a science! She was and is my **SHERO**! Her lessons served me well in various areas of my life and I would often pull out a few of her one-liners to get my point across.

My sisters and I learned so many lessons from our mother and we were never too proud to say "my Momma said..." to anyone who needed a life lesson at that moment. While I attended the school of "Sassy Momma Carol Jean" and absorbed all the character-building lessons I could, there was one lesson I still had yet to learn - how to be that of wife, specifically Mr. Parker's wife. No, this I had to learn through trial and error!

My husband Will and I were 20 years old when we met and we essentially grew up together. At the time I met him, I was engaged to another man. Yes, girl, you heard me. I thought I was marrying another man, but due to God-foreseen circumstances the relationship was thankfully dissolved. Whew! I'm so glad God didn't allow me to go through with that mistake. Unbeknownst to me, the Lord sat my husband right next to me in a Public Speaking college course and the rest is history!

Let me tell you a little bit about the head of my household. On the exterior my husband is burly and solid, but on the interior he has an extremely loving heart. He is hilarious and prides himself on the ability to make me laugh until my sides hurt.

Now, don't let the kind heart fool you! He's not afraid to tell you how he feels about something and he radically protects all things dear to him. He's intelligent, street savvy, and pushes pass the boundaries of conventional tunnel-thinking. He's my comforter, my strength when I'm weak, and my quiet place within a storm. In addition to all that, I was drawn to his scrumptious good looks, dark eyes and long eyelashes. His overall character represented safety and his natural protective instincts fit into the broken places I needed sheltered.

In our dating years, Will and I were inseparable. You didn't see one without the other. When it became apparent that we were in this for the long haul, we put our friends and family on notice; informing them of our new status. Combining our lives meant that the people in our lives were just as invested in this relationship as we were. My wonder twin, Lisa, who was 15 at the time, promptly embraced our relationship and held on tight. She would refer to us as "her" couple. Watching from the sidelines and taking notes for her future relationships, as we lived out our relationship in front of her. She was all in; totally invested, along with the rest of our family and friends.

Will and I were 23 years old when we got married and have been married now for almost 20 years. Like other married couples, we went through many growing pains to get where we are today. We spent a lot of time trying to learn our roles in the relationship and it didn't come easy. I went into my marriage with an independent woman's mindset and a "nobody was going to change what my Momma taught me, not even my husband" attitude. Needless to say, this behavior didn't get me very far before trouble began to erupt in our marriage.

There were things that my husband needed from me to feel respected and appreciated. Unfortunately, I didn't know how to give him those things without feeling like I was compromising the teaching from my upbringing. I remember firmly holding on to the notion that preparing my husband's plate somehow made me a weak and vulnerable woman. Boy, did I have a lot to learn!

During the first few years our marriage went through some serious trials and tribulations. Unfortunately, we experienced infidelity, money management differences and disrespectful treatment toward one another. Not to mention, we were both extremely head strong, which worked for and against us at times. Throughout the course of our relationship, we came to understand what our marriage vows, "for better or for worse" really meant!

During a particularly turbulent season in our marriage, infidelity reared its ugly head and nearly shattered our marriage. My husband and I were not on the same page at all. We'd been married for about five years, but it felt like we didn't know each other anymore. We had turned into two totally different people living two different lives. When everything came out in the open and I had to face the ugly truth of what was happening in our marriage, I was overwhelmed and didn't know what to do or say. When I looked at my husband I saw a man that I loved dearly, but all I felt in my heart was pain. I was confused, disoriented and devastated.

Not knowing what I should do, I just stood there frozen. My self-confidence faded to black and took a back seat to the humiliation I was feeling. All I could think was "I'm not enough for him". Thoughts of self-doubt and unworthiness taunted me and nearly took the wind out of me. I began to think about the countless investors we had in our relationship and how devastated they would be from this news. Then it hit me and I thought dreadfully, "My marriage is over!"

The pain I felt was too much for me to bear and I was frantically searching for a place to store it so that I didn't have to feel it, just as I had done with all the other pain I experienced in my life. In that moment, God told me that this was not my battle to fight. I distinctly remember hearing Him tell me to stay in my marriage and to tell my husband that I wasn't going anywhere.

I hesitated for a moment, but I followed His directions and I heard myself tell my husband that, "I'm not going anywhere". It felt like an out of body experience. I couldn't believe those words came from my mouth because that was not what I was thinking or feeling! I knew that had to be the work of the Lord, because my flesh wasn't strong enough to make that bold decision on its own.

After several lengthy discussions, my husband and I agreed to stay in our marriage and to move forward with our lives. I wanted so badly to move on from this experience as quickly as I could so, I went straight into "fix it" mode. Instead of doing it with the Lord, I tried to do it in my own strength. I told my husband I had forgiven him, when in fact I had done no such thing. I tried to do and say all the right things to make sure that I was making him happy but that didn't work. I began seeking and taking the advice of my friends. That didn't work either. Nothing I tried seemed to ease the pain I was feeling or "fix" the problems in our marriage. I didn't know what to do at this point. I shut down. I couldn't fix it!

I knew my husband was frustrated about how I was showing up in our marriage, but I didn't have the emotional capacity to deal with his feelings at the time. I was growing tired of not being genuinely happy and not being my authentic self, but I still didn't know how to get rid of the pain.

I felt my husband owed me something because I stayed in our marriage. I convinced myself that He needed to show me some big, grand gesture and that would make all the pain go away. Since, he was the one who broke me, he should be the one to fix me, right? Wrong! No matter what my husband could have done, it still would not have been enough. I employed the wrong person for such a big job. Starting to sound familiar?

FIND YOUR FOOTING

After carrying around my "you owe me something" attitude for a couple of years and realizing it wasn't getting me anywhere, I decided it was time for me to spend some time alone with God. In my quiet time with Him I had one of the most profound "Aha" moments of my life. He showed me that I was a prisoner of un-forgiveness! I realized that not only was I being held captive by an unforgiving, broken heart, but I was also holding my husband responsible for healing it.

Instead of giving God my heart to heal, I expected my husband, my protector, to be the healer of all my pain. Yes, the experience of what happened in our marriage was not pleasant and I'm not excusing the behavior, but it was completely unfair to hold him accountable to heal all that was broken in my heart.

Will is the head of my house and the holder of my heart, but the Lord is the *healer* of my heart. I realized that God was telling me (and had been trying to tell me for years) to give Him back His rightful position and release my husband from this heavy burden. While it's great to believe the love between two people can weather the storms that will come against a union created by God, it surely can't be the only thing you need to survive it. God has to be at the head of it all.

Solely relying on yourself or someone else to take on all your feelings and emotions and to "fix" them is simply a setup for disappointment. If you're holding someone hostage for the ransom of your heart, I encourage you to set them free. Release them from the responsibility of healing all the broken pieces in your life and give the Lord back His job. He is more than capable!

After years of trying it "my" way and failing miserably, I finally gave up the fight. **I surrendered it ALL!** It was like someone had flipped a switch in my heart and I began to feel Him again. I fell in love with Jesus and began to fully understand the sacrifice He made for me so that I could have this wonderful, loving relationship with the Father. I made the decision to make Him the head of my life again and totally trust Him. He made me whole again.

I stopped trying to mask, hide and control everything in my life. My prayers changed from "change my husband" to "change me" instead. I prayed for God to restore my marriage and blow new life into it, instead of trying to fix it myself. I prayed *for* my husband and that God would give him the desires of his heart. He did a mighty work in my marriage and He's still doing it every day.

Whatever your reason for putting God on the shelf, it's not big enough for Him to turn away from you. In Luke 15: 11-32, Jesus tells the story of the prodigal son. The point of that story is that even after you've made some poor choices in your life, you can go home again. God's not mad at you. He wants nothing more than for you to run back to Him. He wants to heal you in places that you didn't realize were broken. Find your footing and start walking with Him again.

HE HAS YOUR BACK

Mid-Sunday mornings in my house are special to me. My husband has started a wonderful tradition where we have a mid-morning breakfast after church. We sometimes watch a movie during breakfast, so we affectionately call this time "Flicks and Flaps" (Flaps is short for flapjacks or pancakes...get it? Cute, right?).

One morning while we were about to partake in the delicious breakfast my husband prepared, my youngest son, Malcolm, asked if he could pray over the food this time. Of course my husband and I were happy to grant his request. Malcolm began his prayer with thanking God for all the wonderful things he had done in our lives, the delicious food we were about to eat and all the great things we have been able to do as a family. As he brought his prayer to a close, Malcolm said "And God, thank you for having my back!" I looked at my husband and we both chuckled quietly. We were so proud of his bold and confident prayer.

A few days later I began to think about what my son said to God. To him it was just that simple! God has my back. He's right; God covers us even when we don't feel Him around us. Every time I avoided something that could have caused me great tribulation in my life, God had my back. Every time I tried to go in a direction I wasn't supposed to be going and several barriers were placed in my way, God had my back!

Think about it for just a minute. Any time you are operating in your own strength and you find yourself fighting an uphill battle, God is waiting for you to simply turn to Him and ask Him to guide your steps. He is trying to tell you that He has your back, but you have to fully trust Him. When I think of surrendering everything to God and really letting go and trusting in Him, I'm reminded of a particular trust activity where you free fall backwards, without looking, into someone's arms. That's complete and total trust! That is exactly what God wants from us. Free fall into the Father's arms; let go and let God. He has your back!

WALKING PARTNERS

When each of our boys were of age to ride the school bus, my husband and I sat them down and explained the do's and don'ts that came along with this privilege. We explained the importance of knowing when to exit the bus, being careful not to leave anything behind and the guidelines for walking home. In detail, we discussed how they were responsible for their walking partners and their walking partners were responsible for them. We described how they should stay close to one another so no one gets lost during the walk and run together if danger appeared. By the end of our briefing, the boys understood that to reach their destination they had stay connected to their walking partners and walk or run together.

Look to the left and the right of you. Are you walking with people who will stay close to you so you don't get lost? Will they run with you when you need to outrun storms in your life? Will they go the distance with you to reach your divine destination? If you can answer these questions, with a resounding "yes!", then keep walking and encouraging one another.

On the other hand, if you couldn't confidently answer these questions with a "yes" or had trouble thinking of one person who fit this description, you may need to consider changing your walking partners. That might sound a bit harsh and I realize this is not as easy as it sounds, but it really is necessary to keep you strong in your walk with God.

I have some fabulous, sold-out for Jesus, divas in my life! These sisters aren't afraid to tell me the truth when I need to hear it. They encourage, support and cheer me on through my trials and triumphs. They pray for me when I can't pray for myself. They hold me accountable for the things I say I'm going to do and celebrate with me when I've accomplished them. I mean these ladies are the real deal and I'm so grateful to have them as my walking partners. They fill me up and I'm happy to return the favor when they call.

God places people in our lives who bless us with the gift of their lives. People like the sanctified soldiers in my life, are rare and precious. When you find them, hold on tight; you'll need them. Having a trusted group of people who share your thinking and encourage you in your walk, will help keep you from losing your footing and falling back into old habits.

It's time to sift through your life and make some pretty tough decisions about your current walking partners. Be honest with yourself. Are you getting what you need from your current crew? Are you all on the same page? Or are you uncomfortably walking along side people you have outgrown?

It's time for you to have a candid conversation with your current walking crew about the changes you're making in your life. They may be friends or family members you've been around all your life, which may make it a bit uncomfortable for you. Regardless, you still need to have this conversation. They may surprise you and be very receptive to your new way of living. If they aren't, make peace with it and move forward. You don't have to remove them from your life, but it might mean your relationship may look a little different...and that's ok. Love them where they are in their lives, but don't abandon your walk to maintain the relationships. Be prayerful about this area of your life; God will place people in your life that will confidently walk beside you and courageously run with you.

WALKING ON DIFFERENT PATHS

"Why doesn't my man go to church?" This is one of the most talked about subjects amongst my circle of friends and family members. Sure we come up with our ideas and theories of why some men don't attend church, but by the end of the conversation we are still left with the same question about our man in particular. Many women have people in your life who don't share the same spiritual beliefs or desire for attending church that you do. And for some of you, this reality has become so disheartening that you've put God on the shelf or pressed the pause button on your walk with Him.

Let's keep it real, ladies! If we had it our way, we would have our men next to us at every church service and wrapped around our arms at several church events, right? We keep telling ourselves that this would be the best thing that could happen in our relationship. But when this does not become reality, it can be very frustrating. While it's great to be on the same spiritual page as your loved one, yelling, screaming or calling the man a heathen is not at all going to get him there. That's not only the wrong way to handle it, but it's also very exhausting for both of you.

I realize it can be difficult attending church by yourself and watching other couples come to church faithfully. Believe me, I totally understand. I used to feel the same way when I didn't have my burly man by my side, as I walked through the doors of the church. I kept thinking these people are going to think I lied about having a husband. It would literally make me cringe when people would ask me where he was or say "we have to get him here". Truth be told, I was really annoyed. So, I decided to concoct a plan that would make my husband go to church.

Every Saturday I would think of creative ways to get my husband to church on Sunday. I mean I tried everything! Yes, EVERYTHING! My husband quite enjoyed some of my creative antics, but it just down right exhausted me. Sometimes he would come with me and I would think, "Wow...it worked!". Only to be let down the following Sunday, when he would inform me that he would not be making an appearance.

After many years of stopping and starting my attendance at church, God opened my eyes and gave me new insight. He helped me come to the conclusion that all my efforts to get my husband to church were interfering with my relationship with HIM! I was becoming so consumed with what other people thought and my longing for him to be by my side, that I forgot that a relationship with God wasn't just about going to church. It was about the time that I put in with Him. It was about cultivating and strengthening my walk and prayer life with Him.

I realized that just because my husband didn't go to church regularly, didn't make him any less a child of God than I was. While I believe in regularly attending and connecting with people who share my beliefs, I wasn't "better" or "more blessed" because I attended church. No, not at all. It *did* mean that I was getting what I needed to be stronger in my faith.

My husband knows and loves the Lord, but his relationship with Him is his business. I had to tend to the business of getting my own relationship with the Father.

So, needless to say, I stopped all my crazy antics (ok, some of them remained because they were just down right fun!) and caring about what other people thought about my husband's church attendance record. I pressed forward in my own relationship with the Heavenly Father and solely and happily continued to whisk through the doors of my holy chapel. I no longer badger or nag my husband to go to church with me. I simply extend the invitation and graciously accept his response. What a difference this simple change has made in my life and his!

Some of you have been trying for years to push the men (or family members) in your lives into church or into a relationship with Christ, but with no success. The truth of the matter is that salvation is very personal. Your relationship with God is YOUR relationship. No matter how hard you try you can't push, sweet-talk, trick, coerce or preach people into church or a relationship with Christ! It's God's job to change hearts and it's your job to love the heart your man has right now.

As followers of Christ, we have to win people to Him not beat them over the head until they surrender. Our lives should be so attractive that anybody watching can't help but want what we have. The best thing you can do for your loved one is give them back to the Father and let Him draw them **THROUGH** you (1Peter 3:1-2).

When they see you consistently living your life this way and no longer pressuring them, you'll see a difference. Pray for your man or loved one with all of your heart and soul. You might feel a little lonely at times, but that shouldn't stop you from chasing after the Father. Let God handle the business of drawing His child to Him.

If you stopped walking with God because your man or loved one isn't in a relationship with Him, I encourage you to do some reflecting and ask yourself some tough questions. Ask yourself, what's the worst thing that could happen if you diligently pursued your relationship with God and fully accepted Christ as your savior? But also ask, what's the worst thing that could happen if you don't?

P.A.U.S.E.

Have you ever wished there was a pause button built on your remote control that you could press when you felt the need to take a break from all the hustle and bustle of  your life? I certainly have and I know I'm not alone (it's ok, you can just nod your head...I won't tell anyone). Not that you would check out permanently from your life, but just long enough to catch your breath and regain the strength to keep going! We're so busy taking care of and doing for everyone in our lives that we end up putting ourselves and our spiritual lives last. We may carve out a little time here and there, but it's usually just that - "a little time".

It's important that we feed our spirits and keep ourselves fully charged to continue to give our best to the things we deem important in our lives. At some point we have to stop, take a deep breath and **P.A.U.S.E.**

- **P - Put it down and PRAY!** Whatever it is that you're carrying, put it down. Your concerns, tasks, and people in your life can become heavy and burdensome at times. God wants you to seek Him and cast your cares and worries on Him. He is a big God and He can take whatever you throw His way. Lean into Him and allow prayer to be your path to peace (Psalm 55:22 and Romans 12:12).

- **A - Ask yourself meaningful questions.** What did I do for myself today? What actions did I take to sustain my inner peace? When you have to answer these questions, you really want to have a good response. It helps to hold yourself accountable.

- **U - Use your time wisely.** Your time is very precious, be careful to whom and what you give it to. Where are you focusing your time? Are you paying attention to things that are not worth your time? Eliminate time thieves in your life. The trick here is identifying them. Sometimes we give our time away to people or things and don't even realize it. Don't answer that call or email. Turn your ringer off for a few minutes (or hours). Take your time back!

- **S - Schedule time for yourself.** If you don't you will always fill your day with other things. Carve out at least 30 minutes for yourself per day (I can just hear the gasping now...do it anyway!) This is your uninterrupted time to pray, meditate and reflect. God wants us to take care of our bodies and our minds so that He can use us to do His will. He can't use you for the purposes He has planned for your life, if you're all used up by all the stuff that you constantly carry around daily.

- **E - Encourage yourself.** Philippians 4:13 says "I can do all things through Christ who strengthens me". Finding your strength in God is very powerful and can change the course of your life. In 1 Samuel 30:6, says David encouraged himself in the Lord when he faced an enormous distress. Encourage yourself in the Lord and use the power He gave you to conquer all that life throws your way.

Staying connected and getting into God's presence daily will help you move through your life and overcome barriers that exist to block your path to your destiny. If you've been feeling discouraged because you can't seem to find hours for your prayer life, let yourself off the hook. It's not about the quantity of time that you have to spend with Him; it's more about the quality of time. I encourage you to look for those moments when you're alone. Whether it's taking a long bath, a walk by yourself, driving in the car, it doesn't matter, just find the time and space to **P.A.U.S.E**.

STEAL AWAY

For years I kept saying that I wish I had a space in my home just for me. I have a beautiful bedroom which I share with my wonderful husband. But it wasn't a space where I could just be by myself. I looked around the house and realized that everyone had their own personal space, but me. The boys have their own separate rooms and a TV/Play room and my hubby has his "man cave", where he goes to relax and unwind.

After I pondered on this reality, I became determined to find a space just for me. I started with trying to make a corner in my room, but that didn't work. I started creating living spaces outside on my deck, but the change in Georgia's weather conditions would often send me back in the house. I would sit in my bed to write and read, but that usually ended up with me watching TV or falling asleep. So, finally it occurred to me that the boys had multiple spaces in the house and something was very wrong with this picture! How did they end up with multiple spaces in the house?

DING...DING...DING...I gave it to them!

Well, it was time to reclaim some of this space. And so the "Diva Den" was born! I made an announcement to the men in my household that from now on the TV/Playroom was now Mommy's "Diva Den" and the boys would no longer have open access to this room. To my surprise, they got onboard fairly quickly. For my 41st birthday, my amazing family transformed this space from a toy-filled, catch-all room into my beautiful "Diva Den". This is my space where I get into the presence of God, write, dance, sing, nap and paint my toes! It's a space just for ME!

Some of you may have your very own "Diva Den", while some of you have a sacred corner somewhere in your home. Whatever it is, use it to nurture your relationship with God, recharge your battery and refresh your mind, body and soul. If you don't have a space at all, I encourage you to find one for yourself. It doesn't have to be fancy. It just has to be YOURS!

INVITATION TO CHANGE YOUR WALK

Allowing yourself to be open to what God has in store for you, calls for you to take some intentional steps toward His direction. Depending on where you are in your life, those steps may feel uncomfortable at first but they get easier. It's going to require you to let go of the control you think you have over everything in your life.

Now, I'm not saying that you don't or won't have the ability to make sound decisions in your life. No, I'm saying that when you walk with God and your steps are in line with His divine order, you won't want to make any decision that doesn't involve seeking His wise counsel first! To some this might sound frightening to just completely let go and give the Father control of your life and to others this might sound just completely crazy, but, I **DARE** you to try it!

It's important that I don't make any assumptions when it comes to your walk with God. Some of you reading this book may not have taken the step to begin your walk. If that's you and you're ready to make the next move, please keep reading. What do you have to lose? For those who have let go of the Father's hand and are ready to re-kindle your relationship with Him, this is for you, as well.

All you have to do is invite God to come into your heart

and accept His love for you. If you're still not sure how to do that, I've provided you with a few words to help you begin your walk with Him. It's up to you to say them, believe them and put your total trust and faith in Him.

> *Heavenly Father,*
>
> *I come before you today to thank you for the ultimate gift of your son. I am extremely grateful that you sent Jesus to pay the ultimate price for my sins. I know that I have not always walked a straight path and I've made some unwise decisions in my life. I'm sorry, Father and I ask for your Forgiveness. I ask that you help me to forgive myself. You loved me when I didn't know how to love myself and for that I graciously thank You. Please come into my heart. Change and direct my path and let Your amazing power and love be the source that fuels my every move. Amen*

For those of you who accepted Christ for the first time or re-kindled your relationship, Congratulations! You just made the best move of your life. It's important that you know and really understand that your salvation is much more than reading a prayer. Your job now is to fully trust God and let Him guide your life. Seek Him diligently and let your life be a representation of Christ. Surround yourself with people who share your same beliefs and are followers of Jesus; you'll need the support and encouragement. Your walk will never be the same. Praise God!

oul-Spiration

"It's time to get back up and walk again. Your destination is waiting for you."

Soul-Freeing Questions

1. Describe your current relationship with God. If you're not in a relationship with Him, what's holding you back?

   _____

   _____

   _____

2. What artificial fillers have you put in place of God in your life?

   _____

   _____

   _____

3. What do you need to be paying more attention to in your life? How has God tried to get your attention in these areas?

   _____

   _____

   _____

4. Think about the person you're holding captive to heal your heart. **Write a letter (or email) and release them of this job. When you're ready, send the letter to them (if they're still living).**

5. Think about the person who introduced you to the Lord or encouraged you to renew your relationship with Him. **Write a Thank You letter to that person and explain what God has done in your life since that time.**

6. It's important to identify people in your life who will encourage you in your walk with God. **Who are your walking partners?**

_____

_____

_____

7. How can you go further in your walk with God? Complete the following sentences.

In the next 7 days, I will...

_____

_____

In the next 30 days, I will...

_____

_____

In the next 60 days, I will...

_____

_____

 Be encouraged by John 3:16, 10:10, 14:6 and Romans 3:23

Chapter 5
Breaking Point

Girl, you made it through the first few chapters and you're half way down the road to getting your S.W.A.G. back! I hope you really spent time answering the soul-freeing questions and developing your plan of action because the work truly happens between each chapter.

Before you go on to read the last few chapters of this book, I want to offer some encouragement to those of you who might be a little like me when it comes to finishing books. You might start off strong with reading a great book (yes, I'm assuming that you think this is a great book) and then get totally derailed by other things going on in your life. You might put the book down, never to pick it back up again. Sure, you had great intentions, but life's circumstances won. Don't let that be the case here! If you don't already have a S.W.A.G. partner, now is a good time to get one.

This could be your breaking point. The point where you break the chains of brokenness, bitterness and bondage. The point where you move beyond the stage of regrets and "should've, could've" statements. Your breakthrough may be just on the other side of this page or in between the next two chapters. Don't miss it because you're too busy or you're at an uncomfortable place in your journey. Most importantly, don't walk away because someone in your life has discouraged you and you're asking yourself "what's the point of continuing?" The point is that **YOU** matter and you don't want to miss the opportunities that you'll be able to pursue because you completed this journey.

Don't let time pass you by or hold you back from getting your deliverance. It's your time and it's your turn, and it's no mistake that you're reading this book. Whether you purchased it or it was given to you by a friend, God knew what He was doing when He put it in your hands. The rest is up to you, my friend.

Did I call out all of your excuses? I hope so, but if I missed a few, cross those off your list too! Now, let's get back to the business of getting your S.W.A.G. back! Get your pen and S.W.A.G. Journal ready because the fun is really about to begin.

Chapter 6
Attitude of Gratitude

I wonder what we would see if we all had hidden video cameras attached to us all day. I'm pretty sure the footage of our lives might look a little like that of a person with multiple personalities. One scene may show a cheerful person full of joy and smiling at the world. But, 10 seconds into the video, we might see the same person turn into a nightmare armed with a vehicle and a mean middle finger that's ready to be used when the mood strikes. I'm sure you've seen these people a time or two or you might be one of them...*I'm just saying.*

Admittedly, we've all had some days where our attitudes resembled tornados or roller coasters. Some days it's hard to roll out of bed and face the world with a "can do" attitude when all you want to do is hibernate for the next three months. But, it's when this attitude becomes your consistent pattern of living that it presents a challenge.

By its definition, according to the Merriam-Webster Dictionary, the word attitude means "*a feeling or way of thinking that affects a person's behavior"*. Simply put, what we think and feel is revealed through our attitudes. Technically, our thoughts give power to our attitudes and we give power to our thoughts! So, attitude is really all about choice. We determine what and how we feel about something happening to or around us.

When I was a child I remember holding my breath until I was red in the face or until my Mother slapped me on the back of the head to make me breathe. This was my way of dealing with things that made me mad. Well, as adults, we clearly can't walk around holding our breath because we're going through difficult times. This would just look down-right ridiculous, as do some of the other ways we choose to deal with adversity, tribulations and the storms of life.

Although it might not feel good, the Lord uses our trials to get our attention, to develop us for His purpose and to glorify His great name. And while we may not understand the point or why we were the selected participant, He will never put you through more than you can handle. The question is, how do YOU handle it when you're going through God's school of life? This is where your reaction meets the power of your thoughts and feelings. Depending on what your thoughts and feelings are focused on, your reaction could carry you forward graciously or sink you to the bottom of the pit of despair. It's all about choice.

GRATEFUL, GRATEFUL, GRATEFUL

Have you seen people who approach any situation thrown at them with an invincible attitude and somehow maintain their composure? Don't you want some of what they have? Well, if your attitude isn't in the right place you might feel like throwing something at them. But seriously, when your mind is focused on the Lord and all that He has done for you, your attitude reflects it. That's called an "Attitude of Gratitude".

Dr. Robert Emmons, Researcher and Author of the book *"Thanks! How the New Science of Gratitude Can Make You Happier",* conducted eight years of research on the effects of gratitude. In his findings he discovered that gratitude improves emotional and physical health, and it has the potential to strengthen relationships and communities. Interesting, right? So, basically, the more we focus on being grateful the happier, healthier and more fulfilled we will be in our lives. Think about that for a minute! We can either choose to pace a hole in the carpet from worrying or praise our way to the exuberant life we long to live. There it is again... choice.

As I think about Dr. Emmons astounding gratitude discoveries, I'm reminded of a time when we took our sons 10 and 4 years old to the mall to have Christmas pictures taken. After we waited patiently for our turn, the photographer's assistant called our name and the boys slowly walked to the area where the backdrop and scene props were being put together for their holiday photo shoot. I was fully prepared to work tirelessly and jump around to make my boys smile for this picture.

I looked at the face of my 10 year old son, William, as the photographer began to pose him; he looked as if someone plastered a smile on his face. But he was willing to endure this uncomfortable moment so that his Mommy could get the pictures she so desired. I then looked at my youngest son just as the photographer handed him a brightly colored, beautifully wrapped gift box. His face changed from one of dread to one of joy in 10 seconds flat!

Malcolm's eyes lit up and a smile came across his face

that I couldn't begin to describe. He thanked the photographer and gleamed with extreme excitement as he looked in my direction. I knew that look very well. This is the look he gets on Christmas Day when we hand him a present. He could hardly contain himself! He had no idea what was in that brilliantly wrapped gift box or if there was even anything in it at all, but the mere thought of the possible options that were waiting on the inside of that box, was enough for him!

The amount of joy and gratitude my son demonstrated that day reminded me of the type of attitude we should have every day for the unknown possibilities that the Lord has waiting for us. Simply in awe of Him and with great expectation for what He will do next, we should be ready to offer Him gracious praise because He does above and beyond what we could ever imagine (Ephesians 3:20). The thought of what He has done in my life leaves my mouth hanging wide open in absolute amazement!

If giving praise and showing gratitude will extend the years of my life and weave happiness throughout all my days, I say let the showering of expressive gratitude begin! How long has it been since you extended a heartfelt "thank you" to the Heavenly Father for all that He has done? When is the last time you told significant people in your life how much they mean to you? If you can't remember, then you, my sister, have some overdue "thanking" to do.

DRAINING OR DRIVING?

Have you ever been around someone with a draining attitude? Every time they come around they're telling you the most negative or pitiful stories, or they are consistently unhappy with everything that they experience. You've never heard them utter one positive word or express their gratitude for anything happening in their lives.

If you're constantly encouraging someone or counseling them on what feels like a daily basis, you are dealing with a **DRAINER.** It's simply exhausting! On the other hand, if YOU are constantly talking about all the things that are going wrong in your life and you rely on your friends and family to pick your spirits up, then girl, *you* are a **DRAINER!**

I remember working with a young lady who came to work every day with an issue. I mean EVERY DAY! I would see her in the hallway and would ask her how she was doing (which I sort of regretted asking) and she would go into a long drawn out story about every negative aspect of her life. Being that I'm a natural encourager, I went into encouragement mode and tried to help her find the bright spots in her life.

She would then combat my intentional uplifting statements with more "woe is me" comments. Having a conversation with her was like a tennis match! I was completely exhausted by the end of it and found myself in a bit of slump for the next hour or so. From that experience, I tried keeping a low profile and not making myself such an easy target for her to find.

One day this young lady came into the office and headed straight for my desk. I knew it was her because I recognized the heavy sound of her stomping through the office. She wasted no time. She sat in the chair in my cubicle (which was for clients) as if it were a therapist's office. She began talking about her work projects, the people in the office, and then about her personal life. Not once did she ask how I was doing or what was going on in my life. No, that would have meant she had to take a breath! But, it was at that moment I realized that she was draining every ounce of my energy. She was stealing my joy and I couldn't let this go on for another day.

I stopped her in mid-sentence and asked her had she been listening to herself talk. She looked at me with a slightly confused and irritated facial expression, which almost made me abandon the conversation I was about to have with her, but I decided to press forward because I truly believed she needed to hear what I was about to tell her. I explained to her that every time she had a conversation with me it was always about something negative in her life.

I went on to tell her that she never shared the successes or highlights of her life with me and that it was simply draining. I encouraged her to take a look at how she approached every situation in her life and thoughtfully make a choice on how she was going to deal with them. I was so relieved that I had shared my thoughts with her that I felt this was surely going to be a turning point for her. But, I was wrong! She looked at me with what seemed to be an irritated look on her face, stood up and simply said "Ok" and walked away. I started to go after her and patch up what I had just said to her, but I knew it was best to let her have a moment to decide how she would process this information.

After that conversation, she hardly spoke to me and tried to avoid me like the plague. I knew that I had struck a chord with her, and that she heard me. I was probably the only one who had ever given her that type of feedback about her attitude. So, I knew it was going to take her a little while to understand and accept what I had told her.

About a couple of months later, I saw her in the hallway and I asked her how she was doing and to my surprise she smiled and said "I'm doing very well, How are you?" That made my heart smile. That conversation was one of the most pleasant conversations we've had since I met her. Although, we never revisited our tough conversation, we were able to move forward and have more balanced conversations.

Now, I don't want you to get the impression that we have to be exuding joy at all times or carry around a fake smile plastered to our faces. No, that's not at all what I'm saying. We all go through things in our lives. Our experiences are unique and can create a multitude of feelings. Because we're knee deep in whatever it is we're experiencing at that time we usually don't see how our attitude is impacting those around us. But then again, it's all about how we choose to handle it.

You can either drain the energy from the people around you because they're constantly encouraging and counseling you or your attitude can be the driving force that motivates and positively infects your friends and family.

THE TASMANIAN DEVIL

"You can't be that happy all the time" is what one of my friends said to me when we first met. She would say that she just knew at any moment I was going to turn into someone totally different because nobody could be that bubbly all the time. I used to get such a kick out of her watching and waiting for me to change and to be honest I took it as a compliment. My genuine nature is bubbly and outgoing, but that doesn't mean I don't experience my share of trials and tribulations. I go through things just like everybody else, but how I choose to deal with them is between me, God and a few trusted people in my life.

Now, let me be clear; there used to be a time when this wasn't always the case. While I was genuinely bubbly and outgoing, my attitude, when provoked, used to resemble that of the "Tasmanian Devil" cartoon character (If you're old enough to remember this Looney Tune's cartoon, you'll get the picture). Picture an animal-like character with sharp teeth, long hairy arms and a disturbing growl. To make it even more interesting, the "Tasmanian Devil" would spin so fast that he would burrow a hole in the ground. Sounds pretty scary, right? Well, that was me!

While, I don't have sharp teeth or long hairy arms, I did growl, "spin off", turn red and nearly bust a blood vessel from yelling at the top of my lungs to get my point across. I wouldn't react like this with everyone in my life and it didn't happen all the time. This "Tasmanian Devil" attitude would usually show up when I felt scared, not in control of a situation or couldn't "fix" something or someone I deeply cared for. The two people who were usually on the receiving end of the "Tasmanian Devil's" spin-off were my husband and my oldest sister, Shonda.

I love my sister, Shon (as I call her), very much. I have always admired her impeccable fashion sense. She is extremely creative and can put together an outfit with a snap of her fingers. She is a Diva! We're only 2 ½ years apart so I was in the receiving line when it came to her handing down the clothes she no longer wanted. To say the least, my wardrobe was pretty spectacular!

Back in the day my sister and I used to hang out quite a bit. We would go to the hottest house parties, hang with some of the "coolest" people and sneak into the most happening clubs. I thought I was so cool when she allowed me to roll out with her. Wherever we went people recognized that I was Shon's little sister and I wore that title proudly.

Being that we're so close in age, sometimes we grooved to the same beat, while other times we were like oil and water. I can recall many fights and arguments when we were younger, but she was always my big Sis and nobody could mess with her while I was around! As we got older our fights changed from the wind milling, hair pulling, nail scratching physical fights to verbal assaults and tongue lashings.

When she first moved to Georgia, my sister came to my house and we were ecstatic to see one another. After a few hours of chatting and catching up on our lives, she made a comment that I didn't agree with and we ended up in a full on verbal sword jousting. The "Tasmanian

Devil" showed up on the scene and before I knew it I was beet red and yelling at the top of my lungs. When she left I stood there in disbelief thinking "I can't believe my sister is still able to push my buttons." I thought I had out grown that behavior.

It wasn't until I came into a closer relationship with God that I realized the "why" behind my "spin- offs" with my sister. He revealed to me that I was carrying around feelings of anger and frustration because I couldn't control what happened to my sister or the effects that it had on all of us. No matter how hard I tried and how loud I yelled, I felt like *I* couldn't "fix" it for her! I couldn't get back for her what I thought she lost and in turn I felt like I had lost. In the midst of all the pain that was experienced, I felt like I lost my big sister.

Unfortunately, trauma has tentacles that can reach far beyond the confines of your own mind, and it can have a negative impact on various areas of your life. The traumatic incident my sister and I experienced earlier in our lives, found its way right into the center of our relationship. I turned the hurt that I was feeling into angry darts and fired them in her direction every chance I got. My attitude was hurting someone I loved and was keeping me from reaching greater altitudes in my life. That was a huge eye- opener for me!

After my revelation, I set out to change my attitude. I intentionally focused my efforts on trusting the Lord and giving Him control over this area in my life. Knowing that my anger really wasn't about my sister, but really more about what I thought I lost, helped me to be aware of my attitude in her presence. Today, our conversations sound and look differently and we now experience more times where we're grooving to the same beat.

As the months went on and my attitude was consistent, Shon jokingly said to me, "You don't "spin off" like you used to". Her words were like music to my soul. I smiled and said "He changed my life". I was so grateful that she could see the evidence of the changes the Lord had made in my attitude.

The moment I gave all of my life to the Lord, the "Tasmanian Devil" ceased to exist. I realized that "spinning- off" was not me gaining control or power, it was me losing it. When I'm able to walk away from an issue I would normally fight tooth and claw to "fix", I feel extremely powerful. I re-gained my power.

Where is your "Tasmanian Devil" attitude showing up? Take a deep breath, sit still for a minute and think about this question. If you recognized yourself through my story or you find your attitude has animal-like characteristics, it's time to take a closer look at the "why".

REPRESENT HIM

As parents, most of us feel like our children are a direct representation of us and if they're publicly acting like they've lost their minds, then we feel it reflects poorly on our parenting skills. It's our desire that our children behave the way we teach them whether we're in public or behind closed doors. Well, we all know that this is simply not the case at all times. The moment your child does something that goes against everything you've been drilling in their heads, you just want to shrink back into the darkest corner until the ridiculousness has stopped. At least that's how I've felt when my two beautiful boys' lively personalities landed them in predicaments that made me cringe. From Malcolm's quick-witted joke telling in the middle of a school lesson to William's obsessive need to correct other students to ensure they were following the rules, my parenting muscles have been stretched on several occasions.

My first reaction is usually to deny that my boys are even capable of any type of behavior other than what my husband and I have instilled in them. Then, after I snap back to reality, I realize that it's truly one of my seedlings exhibiting some form of displeasing behavior, and the embarrassment settles right in the pit of my stomach. Sound familiar?

Picture this scene. A child throws an all-out fit in the middle of a store because things aren't going their way. I'm sure you've either seen this situation or experienced it. What's the first thing you think when you see this happening? Well, if you're like me, you're probably thinking (as you discreetly stare) how grateful you are that it's not you and wondering how they're going to handle this tragic situation.

Will they handle it gracefully or will they blow up right there in aisle 6? However the unruly behavior is handled, it'll probably include a stern enough consequence to hopefully ensure the child doesn't embarrass the parent like this ever again in the future. After all, their reputation is on the line!

The same holds true for us as children of The King. We have a responsibility to uphold His impeccable reputation and to be obedient to His perfect Will. God's reputation is at stake when we freak out or simply lose it when things don't go our way. Don't get me wrong; the Father is perfect in every way and His Name alone commands respect. But, as His children, we represent Him through how we live our lives. God created us to glorify Him not just when we feel good, but in ALL that we go through.

When we profess to be a part of the body of Christ that means we've signed up to be a representative for the Almighty. But, just because I call myself a follower of Christ doesn't mean my words or my attitude reflect it. I could be dressed and draped from head to toe with bejeweled crosses and "Soldier for the Lord" pins. But, my attitude could resemble that of a hellion, ready to fire off a verbal assault that you never saw coming. My attitude should match my Christ-like wardrobe.

I imagine if there was a job description for this role it might look something like this:

JOB TITLE: Representative of The Almighty

Purpose: Represent the reputation of The Almighty and glorify His name.

Job Duties:
(Note: The Almighty can adjust the degree of these duties at any time.)

- ✓ Trust in the Lord God with all your heart
- ✓ Consistently seek God through prayer
- ✓ Love, love, love
- ✓ Believe what God says about you
- ✓ Accept forgiveness and forgive others
- ✓ Encourage others through your testimony
- ✓ Prepare your lap for an out pouring of blessings
- ✓ Be confident in who God created you to be
- ✓ Use your gifts and talents to glorify The Almighty
- ✓ Live an abundant life
- ✓ Smile and laugh often

Work Environment Will Require You:

- ✓ Lift your hands in praise.
- ✓ Lay your burdens down.
- ✓ Put on the full armor of God
- ✓ Experience unconditional love from The Almighty.

<u>Perfect people need not apply!</u>

Sign me up, flaws and all! Would you apply? I believe we can all qualify for this job if we want to be followers of Christ. How we carry out the duties will show up in our performance review with the Boss!

Just as we expect our children to be obedient and to "act like they have some sense" in public, the same is expected of all of us. If I'm doing my job correctly, people watching should see me striving to display Christ-like behavior throughout my day-to-day living. My inside should match my outside. My attitude should be so infectious that it will influence those around me to sign up for the job of representing The Almighty.

ATTITUDE ADJUSTMENT

For years my Mother has described the consequences of the spine being out of alignment and the benefits of getting it adjusted. She explained that when your spine is out of alignment then your balance can be altered and various muscles in your body can be weakened. Thinking about her wise warnings, I began to think how this compares to our attitudes. When our attitudes are not aligned with the Father, the balance in our lives is altered and over time we find that many areas breakdown and become weakened. Before we know it we are in dire need of an attitude adjustment!

I want you to stop and think about your attitude. Think about the last time you were faced with a challenge in your life. How did you show up? Did your thoughts run wild and have you behaving like a whirlwind or did you approach it with an optimistic outlook? Think about your everyday dealings with friends and family. How would they say you show up? Would they rate your attitude as one that is to be admired or one to be avoided? Would they consider you to be a "drainer" or "driver"? Or are you showing up with your "Tasmanian Devil" attitude in full throttle?

Our attitudes are powerful and can *really* get us into some outstanding opportunities or some pretty astounding messes! The good news is that you have a choice. You can choose to let your thoughts and feelings control you or you can get control of them. You're in charge of how you receive information and how you deliver it, and you have the ability to take charge of your attitude at any moment and turn it around.

Throughout this chapter you may have recognized some attributes of your own attitude and identified areas for adjustment. To help get you started, here are a few tips that helped me adjust my attitude.

1. **Be Prayerful** – Ask God to help change your attitude and align your thoughts with His perfect Will for your life.

2. **Be Grateful** – Look back over your life and recognize all the times God has seen you through situations. Praise Him for all that He has done for you and begin praising Him for all that He has yet to do for you.

3. **Be a Blessing** – Focus your thoughts on blessing someone else. When you use what God has given

you to bless someone else, your thoughts begin to shift and your attitude will be changed because of it. It's hard to think about your troubles when you're thinking about blessing someone else.

4. **Believe** – What God says about you is true. Remind yourself who you are and WHOSE you are on a daily basis. Immerse yourself in His Word so that it's imprinted on your heart. Find a few scriptures that speak to your heart.

5. **Breathe** – Our thoughts and feelings can sometimes consume us and leave us holding our breath or gasping for the next one. Take a deep breath and exhale. This helps you clear your mind so you're able to hear clearly from God.

Much like spinal adjustments, you'll want to revisit and consider making regular adjustments to your attitude to keep it in proper alignment.

Soul-Spiration

"Everything we do comes from our heart (Proverbs 4:23). Your mouth speaks what's in your heart. What fills your heart?"

Soul-Freeing Questions

1. What words best describe your attitude?

_____

_____

_____

2. How do you think your friends and family would describe your attitude?

_____

_____

_____

3. Ask three friends or family members to describe your attitude. Capture their responses.

_____

_____

_____

4. Identify three adjustments you would like to make to your attitude (and make them).

_____

_____

_____

5. Call or write a letter to the most important or influential person in your life and share with them how they have impacted your life.

6. Create a Gratitude Journal. On a weekly basis, write down at least one thing you're grateful for and share it with your S.W.A.G. partner.

7. Think about the attitude adjustments you identified in question 4 and describe the actions you will take to make these a reality.

In the next 7 days, I will...

_____

_____

In the next 30 days, I will...

_____

_____

In the next 60 days, I will...

_____

_____

 Be encouraged by Ephesians 4:31-32, Romans 12:2 and Galatians 5:22-23

Chapter 7
God-Given Gifts & Talents

So far you've thoughtfully examined your self-confidence, your walk with God and your attitude. You were challenged to re-visit some past experiences and answer some tough questions that, hopefully, provoked you to action. Next, we're going to look at your gifts and talents; the stuff God gave you to give the world!

This chapter not only follows the first few chapters because it's the last letter in the word S.W.A.G., but also because you can't begin to walk in your gifts and talents until you've re-gained your confidence, restored your walk with God and renewed your attitude. These are the very attributes that prepare you to showcase them to the world. Your self-confidence is what helps you stand upright in your gift. Your walk with God will keep you upright and your attitude will help propel you to where God wants you to be. If we lack in any of these areas then attempting to walk in our gifts can be an agonizing process.

We all have gifts and talents that were given to us by the Heavenly Father. When we're not confident enough to use them, they go unrecognized and lie dormant where no one can see them. That is not at all why He placed those gifts inside each of us. It's time to wake them up!

THE AWAKENING

Chances are you play many roles in your life. You probably play leading roles such as: mom, wife, sister, daughter, employee, business owner, mentor and countless other roles. At any given time, you probably operate in some of these roles simultaneously. (Whew! I'm exhausted just thinking about it!) As you operate in these roles on a daily basis, giving, providing, nurturing; it's so easy to forget the one important role that keeps all these roles functioning - SELF!

Because of our nurturing nature, we often forget that we have a purpose outside of meeting everyone else's needs. We put this immense pressure on ourselves to be great at every role, leaving little space and time to carry out our heart's desires or the plan that God has for OUR lives.

Now, I'm not saying that you should ignore the various roles you play in your life to run off and live your dreams! No, I'm saying that you simply can't forget about you and what defines your purpose. YOU matter!

120

Being *submissive* to the roles that you play in your life doesn't mean being *dismissive* to the gifts and talents God placed in you. According to 2 Timothy 1:6 we are to stir up the gifts inside of us. Simply put, we are to use what has been given to us to impact others. You may have tucked away some unfinished projects or suppressed some amazing visions because of doubt, fear or unforeseen circumstances in your life. Or you just got ridiculously busy and created a barrage of excuses for your lack of zeal! Right? Well, it's time to shake the doubt, quiet the voice of fear, dump the excuses and awaken those gifts that are longing to be used.

If you listen to the voice of doubt long enough, you'll convince yourself that you don't deserve what God gave you. He didn't give you that gift to hide it or be afraid to use it (Matthew 25:14-30). He gave it to you to glorify Him and to touch the lives of others. So, let's get moving.

GIFT CONNECTION

Think back to the last time you were given a great opportunity or the last time you were given something that changed your life. Who was on the other side of that opportunity or life changing situation? A friend, a family member or perhaps a stranger from a chance meeting? As I said earlier, God places people in our lives for a reason, season or a life time. That means that we're all connected. He created us to live together, learn together and grow together.

We have a great responsibility to live our lives unselfishly helping each other. That's a pretty big deal, wouldn't you say? When we fully use the gifts that God gave us, we help someone else use theirs. I'm honored and to tell the truth, a little giddy, when God uses me to help someone walk in their gifting. It may not always be on a stage or a large platform that He uses me, it might be simply from the padded seat of my office chair or the bathroom in the grocery store. Whenever He decides to tap into my gift, I respond. In the same respect, God has placed many people in my life to release the gifts in me.

About five years ago God began tugging on me to do something bigger than myself. Instead of ignoring this tugging or explaining it away, I listened to His voice. I began excitedly searching for my assignment, not knowing that God had already found one for me. A familiar organization came to the top of the list on a volunteer match site that I was diligently searching. He led me to Diamond in the Rough (DITR), a girls' mentoring and leadership development program. I just laughed to myself and said "Ok, Lord, you are up to something".

I'd been introduced to this amazing organization a few years prior, but was unable to volunteer at that time because I was pregnant with my youngest son. I was immediately intrigued by the bold Mission Statement that nearly jumped off their website. It read: *"Transforming the world, one child...one family...one community at a time".* Wow, the Lord thought enough of me to include me in such an immense, fearless and world-changing vision! I was honored, but still a little unsure how I would fit into this organization.

I immediately contacted the organization and was put in contact with the Founder and Executive Director, Nicole Steele. I listened intently, as she explained their needs and that they were looking for a Trainer to step in and train new volunteer mentors. I just closed my eyes and smiled, it was His final confirmation.

Training, developing and encouraging adults was not only my career field, but also my passion.

After hearing Nicole explain the requirements of the volunteer role of Trainer, I have to admit I was a little nervous about the time commitment, but I thought to myself "I can do this." I will simply just volunteer on a small scale and that will fulfill my assignment. Ha! God had a different agenda. He wanted me to use my gifts on a larger scale. I had no idea what He had planned for me.

I came into the DITR organization thinking I would just be a volunteer Trainer whenever there was a need, but again that was MY plan. I fell in love with this organization, the girls, the volunteers and the overall mission. As Nicole branched out more and more, I found myself planted right there in the midst of it all. This was the Lord's plan all the time.

After five amazing years serving in this organization, I'm now the Director of Training and Development, a Youth Mentor and I wear any other hat I'm called to wear. Because God connected me to one of His daughters who is fiercely walking in her gift, not only am I walking upright in my gifts, but through this organization, I've been given opportunities and platforms which have stretched them.

I'm sincerely grateful to my friend, Nicole, for being obedient to the call on her life and confident enough to provide me a platform to showcase my gifts and talents. When you know you have an assignment on your life, you won't hesitate to use what you've been given by the Father. You have no idea who you're setting free to impact the world, when you're obedient enough to use yours.

IF THE GIFT DON'T FIT, DON'T WEAR IT!

My sisters and I are a lot alike in various ways; especially my youngest sister, Lisa, and I. We talk alike, find humor in the same things, share the same profession and have even been mistaken for one another. But there are two key areas where we differ. Our height and our feet! While we love some of the same styles in shoes, we've never been able to swap shoes. She would be trying to fit her foot into a shoe that would squeeze, pinch and cause her excruciating pain. While I would look downright ridiculous and probably fall flat on my face trying to wear shoes that would flop right off my feet. This is what we look like when we try walking in someone else's gift, instead of walking in our God-given gifts.

Some of us are so busy trying to walk in someone else's gift, that we never fully do what we were called to do. If God wanted us to be our best girlfriend or co-worker, He would've just made us that person, right? It's fine to admire someone's gifts and talents and to take pointers from them, but the moment you start trying to be that person and put on her gift, that's where it all goes wrong, sister!

Each of our gifts are custom tailored to fit us. Like anything custom-designed, it naturally fits you and feels right. Trying to do something that doesn't fit you, won't feel natural and may end up hurting you. Like a pair of shoes you know you should never have bought in that smaller size (because they were the last pair); they simply just don't fit! You know what I'm talking about!

We're all important to the Lord and He can and will use each and every one of us, if we let Him. Whatever God called YOU to do, IS significant. Some of us are called to be Moms, some of us are called to be professionals, entrepreneurs, and some are called to be supporters and encouragers. Stop comparing yourself to other people, especially other women. Encourage, support and cheer your "sister" on while she's walking in her gift and be confident enough to walk in your own.

"DO" SEASON

"I got it!" I said when God revealed what He wanted me to do with the gift that He had given me. It was crystal clear and I was so excited. I started looking for any opportunity to use my gift. It was like my son, Malcolm, when he received his first foam dart gun. He would fire at everything that looked like it could hold the suction of the darts. That was how I felt with the gift that God revealed to me. Ready...Aim...Fire!

Since my college years, I knew that I thoroughly enjoyed motivating adults. It's something about watching people get that "Ah Ha" moment when something clicks for them, that makes my heart melt. For more than 18 years I've been able to design and facilitate training sessions and workshops where I get to see people have this experience. But it wasn't until God confirmed for me that this was the gift that He gave me to give the world that I really got excited. I began to look for every opportunity to start using my gift and one presented itself, or so I thought!

A friend of mine interviewed my distant cousin who lived in California. I learned that he conducted various, highly-attended, motivational workshops and after connecting with him, he invited me to attend one of his workshops if I was ever in California. Well, it just so happened that the company I worked for asked me to facilitate a workshop in California, in the same area. I just knew that this was a sign from God. It was perfect! I called my cousin to tell him the good news and began making plans to extend my business trip to be in attendance at his workshop. BAM! It was done. "It's really happening. I'm going to walk in my destiny!" I thought to myself.

It wasn't until I looked at the discontent on my husband's face, who had overheard my phone conversation that I realized what I had done. I had not even thought of including him in MY plans for my extended visit to California. Not only did I not include him, but I didn't think to ask for his thoughts. He was less than pleased and made sure to express his thoughts. I was so excited about what I thought God was doing in that season that I didn't even stop long enough to discuss it with one of the most important people in my life. "Did I get it wrong? Isn't this what God wants me to do? Isn't this my "Do" season?" I thought to myself.

Well, just as God would have it, the company cancelled my business trip to California and it was never rescheduled. God shut it all the way down! I believe that was His way of saying "Pump your breaks, child, I did not tell you to DO anything, yet!" Sometimes we can get ahead of God and think that we are hearing from Him; when actually we're being led by our own thoughts.

When God calls you to do something the doors will open right up and you will flow right into whatever He has called you to do, just like that! But, when it's not of Him you may stumble, trip or take an unfortunate fall through those doors and end up with a not so pleasant scar that shows up in your life. And that's not cute, ladies!

It's exciting to know what your gifts and talents are, but it's also foolish to use them before God has prepared you. That doesn't mean that you sit on your gifts and miss what God is telling you to do. No, it just means that you need to seek His wise counsel before diving in head first. Our gifts may be used in different seasons of our lives. This may be your preparation season. The season where the Lord is preparing you for what He has in store. It's my belief that if we try to use our gifts out of season, it could potentially hurt us or the people around us.

There's no telling what would've happened if I had attended my cousin's workshop and received certification to teach it. What damage could MY decision have done to my marriage or the people in my life? Would I have heard God tell me to write this book? Well, I'm glad that the Lord stepped in and cancelled MY plans. That was not my "Do" season. I'm so glad God doesn't always give us what WE want. He knows what He's doing!

STUCK

Have you ever had your car stuck in the mud or snow? I have a time or two and let me tell you it's not a fun experience! Being from the Midwest, I've experienced my share of driving in the snow, sliding in the sleet and walking through some pretty thick mud. But, there is truly nothing like getting your car stuck in a mound of mud covered snow. No matter how hard you try, your wheels just keep spinning and spinning; only making matters worse. Your only saving grace is a kind stranger who comes along to give you a push to help get you on your way.

Some of you might have found yourselves stuck in a mound of your own. You might've tried a few ventures, but nothing has seemed to stick. Or you keep "spinning your wheels" trying unsuccessfully to identify your gifts. You may have even started down your destiny path, but stopped because life happened or a barrier presented itself. Sometimes, all it takes is a little push to get us going in the right direction.

That push might come in the form of a friend or family member's encouraging words or challenge for you to try a different approach to something. It might come in the form of an opportunity that you might normally turn down. It could also come from a complete stranger who was sent just to give you the help you need.

God knows what we need and when we need it. He has a way of showing us signs regarding the very area where we're stuck. Our challenge is not being too busy, too distracted or too proud to see the signs. If this is starting to sound eerily familiar to you, then, girl, I encourage you to take a moment and think about the many signs that God sent to push you from your stuck position. Are you beginning to remember a few pushes? If so, good.

Now, I'm going to give you a little push. Yep, that's right; right here and now. Writing your wildest dream or vision without limits will sometimes help you identify your gifts and talents. It can also help you move from complacent to creative. Are you ready to take the limits off and get out of that mound that you've been stuck in? Great, let's go!

I want you to close your eyes (well, after you read the rest of the activity) and think about what you would do if there was no possibility that you could fail. Think about where you're at in your life and what you would love to be doing. Got it? Ok, now in the space provided below, or in your S.W.A.G. Journal, finish the statement.

If there were no limitations in my life, I would:

_____

_____

_____

_____

_____

_____

_____

_____

_____

_____

_____

_____

_____

_____

_____

_____

_____

_____

_____

_____

Now, carefully look at what you wrote and identify areas where you're currently using skills that could get you to your dream.

_____

_____

_____

_____

_____

_____

_____

Last, but certainly not least, identify people in your life who have either given you a push or can currently give you a push in the right direction.

_____

_____

_____

_____

_____

_____

_____

_____

_____

_____

Finding or re-discovering your gifts is an exciting journey. Hopefully, you were able to identify a few key nuggets in your writing. What you do with those nuggets is now up to you. If you weren't able to complete this exercise, don't be discouraged, try it again at a later time.

If you're still searching for your gifts and talents, I encourage you to spend some alone time with God. He will reveal where He placed them. You'll be reminded of the many times God used your gifts, even when you didn't recognize it. You may not have had a big platform or stage, but your life has trails and imprints of your gifts all over it. Think about your daily interactions with people, your job, your personal relationships and your children. You've touched, blessed and encouraged people along the journey of your life. That, my sister, is a pretty powerful gift.

Our gifts have seasons, yours might be right now. It's time to turn some heads and do some pretty incredible things with your life. Don't miss your season because you've put limitations on yourself.

IT'S NOT TOO LATE

Have you ever made a list of the things you wanted to do or see before you die? Ok, think about that list (if you don't have a list, think about all the things you have been saying that you want to do). How many things on your list have you actually completed (and "No", just signing up for an activity on the list does not count!)? If you've accomplished several things on your list, CONGRATULATIONS! Keep going and make a new list. If you're looking at your list and shaking your head because it looks pretty much the same as the day you wrote it, then you my friend have some explaining to do but, don't worry, you're not alone!

What's holding you back? Why haven't you made steps to crossing off some of those wonderful experiences on your list? There will always be "things" or "stuff" we need to get done. And there will never be the "perfect" time to do all the things we desire to do. So, why keep putting them off? While it's important to make responsible decisions in the way we live our lives, it's also important to be an active participant in it.

You may be thinking that you've run out of time to use your gifts & talents. Not true! It's never too late. Ok, well maybe when you're no longer amongst the living population. But, as long as you have air flowing through your lungs, you still have time. That doesn't mean you need to hurry up and make up for lost time by doing some outlandish things God didn't ask you or purpose you to do. Girl, please don't do that! No, it means that God can still use you and that you are still significant to Him.

Abraham and Sarah both thought it was too late for them to have a child and look what God birthed from those two (Genesis 18:11-14). Don't let your age, circumstances, or your mind hold you back from unveiling your greatness. You still have time to dust off your big ideas, visions and dreams and put them into action. In the words of a well-known English novelist and poet, Mary Ann Evans (more well-known by her pen name George Eliot), "It's never too late to be what you might have been.", and I couldn't agree with her more.

My oldest son, William, is truly one of my biggest encouragers. This became very evident during one particular summer when he joined a track team for the first time. I was super excited for him! Anyone who knows me knows that track was my sport of choice.

From elementary to high school, you could always find me on the track field. I was all about getting out there on the track and competing to bring home a shiny, 1st Place medal. So, when my son decided to give it a try, I was fully prepared to cheer him on from start to finish!

Well, being the encouraging son he is, William decided to sign me up for the parent/coach 4 x 100 relay team at one of his track meets (yes, he signed me up!). At first I resisted and tried talking myself out of it several times but that voice of passion, which I thought went away when I was 17 years old, kept tugging at me. Well, I decided to listen to that voice and to William, who kept egging me on so I dusted off my track shoes.

The day of the race finally arrived and I have to admit I was nervous and excited all at the same time! After praying over all my limbs (and a lot of stretching), I took my position on the track marker and "Bang", the starting gun went off! It was one of the most exhilarating feelings I'd felt in a long time.

There I was, waiting for my teammate to hand off the baton and hearing the cheers from my husband and my son. This was my opportunity to show them the talents I had in my glory days. And my chance to live in my passion one more time. My heart was thumping and I prayed that I would have the strength and the courage to do the best I could. After all, it had been 23 years since I stepped foot on a track to compete.

Words can't explain how it felt to have that baton placed in my hand and to take off down the track in hopes of beating my competition! **IT WAS TRULY AMAZING!** My team came in 3rd place, but we all felt like we had just won the Olympic gold medal. It was a true accomplishment and one that changed the game for me. "I did something that I never thought that I could do again; what else am I capable of doing?" I thought.

As I was sitting on the ground stretching my legs, I stared intently at my running shoes. I decided at that very moment that I was trading in my shoes of self-doubt and fear for a pair that would exude the boldness and confidence the Lord replaced in me. From that point in my life, I knew that if I could get my old behind out there and run a race that could've put me on the sidelines for good, then I could confidently and boldly do the things that God was asking me to do.

So, to all of you list makers that are sitting on your lists (Bucket, 30 by 30, 40 by 40, 60 by 60, etc.), get up, revitalize your list and get to living! If you need to make a few tweaks to get some early wins, do it! It's time to change the game! Shake off the weight of all that has been holding you back. Shut off the noise of those around you telling you that you can't do "it"; whatever that "it" is in your life. It's not too late to trade in those shoes of self-doubt for a shiny, brand new pair to start walking (or running) in your gift. Imagine the possibilities.

HANDLE WITH CARE

When we wrap a gift for someone we care about we put time and effort into it. We thoughtfully select beautiful wrapping paper, a fancy gift bag or box. We adorn it with a perfectly tied bow or satin ribbon. Then we get it ready for presentation; hoping that the décor is just as pleasing as what is inside the package. Finally, a thoughtful expression of our feelings is written to the gift receiver, explaining how we were moved or touched by them. We do all this in preparation of delivering this amazing gift.

If we think about our God-given gifts in the same manner as the beautifully wrapped present, then we'd realize that we need to make the same careful and thoughtful efforts before presenting our gifts to the world. God intended us to use our gifts to build and edify His Kingdom, but when they're not handled with care you won't be able to fulfill this duty.

Caring for our gifts includes being mindful of who we present them to and where and how we use them. God didn't intend for us to use our gifts and talents in places or on people that will not respect or appreciate them (Matthew 7:6). No matter how determined we are to use our fabulous gifts, we should never use them in any way that would bring shame to ourselves or misrepresent His glory.

Our gifts should be protected, strengthened and built up until it's time to deliver them to the receiver. What are you doing to protect, strengthen, or further build your gifts? Will you be ready and prepared to present them when the time comes? If your answer is no, I encourage you to begin putting a plan in place to hone your gifts. I'm sure many of the world's greatest singers have a regimen they follow to protect, strengthen and improve their voices until their next big performance. Invest in what has been entrusted in you. Don't wait until God has called you to perform to start working on your gifts. Start now! Practice, prepare and perform in front of an audience of one...yourself! Do what it takes to stay ready, so you don't have to get ready when it's your "DO" season. Whatever your gifts are, be a wise steward over them; after all, your Daddy gave them to you!

oul-Spiration

"Don't miss your "DO" season because you've placed limitations on your possibilities."

Soul-Freeing Questions

1. What projects or visions have you tucked away? Why?

_____

_____

_____

2. Think about the writing activity you completed in this chapter. What insights did you gain from this activity?

_____

_____

_____

3. What barriers do you need to remove to begin using your gifts and talents?

_____

_____

_____

4. If at all, describe the areas where you are stuck and why?

_____

_____

_____

5. What "push" do you need to get unstuck?

_____

_____

_____

6. How will you protect, strengthen and hone your gifts?

_____

_____

_____

7. Describe the actions you will take to begin walking in your gifts and living without limits.

In the next 7 days, I will...

_____

_____

In the next 30 days, I will...

_____

_____

In the next 60 days, I will...

_____

_____

 Be encouraged by 1Peter 4:10, Matthew 5: 14-16 and 2Timothy 1:6

Chapter 8
Take Action

My husband is always telling our boys that paying attention to details is imperative because you don't want to miss anything significant. I took that to mean when you miss the minor details, the major ones get overlooked. For years I missed the details sprinkled throughout my life that warned me to pay attention. It wasn't until I made a conscience effort to go back and trace these details, that I got my S.W.A.G. back.

I was committed to doing the work it took for me to finally be free. I fought for my freedom. It's time for you to rise up from the corner that's holding you captive and come out swinging and fight for the life you deserve to live. It's a rewarding process I encourage you to embrace.

Writing this book further helped me to recognize the journey the Lord had me on. As I was writing, I felt His presence ministering to my soul and cleaning out any residue that might have been left behind. I am no longer bound by fear, doubt and pain. I can confidently and boldly say that I know that God has a glorious plan for me. He was waiting for me to finally realize it.

The information in this book is probably not unlike what you've heard from others. Hopefully, you were reminded of some conversations you've had or advice you were given by a trusted friend or family member. It's my prayer that you will think of this book as your warm embrace from the Father, telling you it's time to get back what you lost. Girl, it's time.

At the beginning of the book, I asked you to write a commitment letter to yourself. If you didn't write it, now is a good time to do it. This letter is written to **YOU**, by **YOU** and for **YOU**. What you've committed to doing to get your S.W.A.G. back is now up to you to complete. If you do nothing, you can probably expect the same results in your life before you began this journey. I encourage you to not only act, but start now, while you're in the moment.

The formula to getting your S.W.A.G. back is unique to each individual and already lies on the inside of you. It's up to you to activate it.

Here are a few things to help you along the way:

- ✓ Through prayer, seek God's help and comfort during your journey. Don't go on this journey without Him.

- ✓ Spend time in God's Word to uplift your soul.

- ✓ Examine your situation and determine what changes you can start making in your life right now.

- ✓ Be patient, prepared and prayed up in your journey.

- ✓ Don't get discouraged if some things you try don't work for you. Try something else. Only God is one size fits all!

- ✓ Find a S.W.A.G. partner and a trusted support system.

- ✓ Listen to the counsel of others who have successfully completed this journey.

- ✓ Keep a journal. Write down your feelings and thoughts as you go through this journey. It's amazing to look back and see your growth.

- ✓ Revisit your answers to the soul-freeing questions within this book.

- ✓ Look for other encouraging resources that will help you on your journey.

- ✓ Visit www.deyonneparker.com and share your experience about your journey. Your testimony and courage just might set someone else free.

There will always be trials and tribulations in life, but when you get your S.W.A.G. back you'll be ready to face them head on. You'll be courageous enough to leap into the amazing plans that God has waiting for you and strong enough to stay there. You'll have the attitude that will make strangers want to bless you. And most importantly your walk with the Father will be so strong and so beautiful people will be drawn to the light they see in you.

I know the Lord is still working in my life every day and I look forward to seeing how my future unfolds in His hands. Through this book, I pray that God will use my past experiences to help set someone else free. I hope that someone is you!

Soul-Spiration

"You've tried the alternatives, now it's time to get your S.W.A.G. back!"

References

Diamond in the Rough, Youth Development Program, Inc. – www.ditr.org

Merriam-Webster Dictionary

The Confident Woman, Joyce Meyers

Thanks! How the New Science of Gratitude Can Make You Happier, Dr. Robert Emmons

YouVersion Bible App – NIV, KJV

oul-Spirations

The Soul-Spirations, inspirational messages to uplift and inspire your soul, found throughout this book were written with you in mind. Write them down on a sticky note and place them on a mirror, a cubicle wall or even on your computer. Somewhere that you can easily see and be encouraged by them.

- "Take back the life you were created to live and shed those past hurts; God wants to replace it with joy!"

- "Free yourself from the shackles of fear and confidently step out on the platform God gave you."

- "It's time to get back up and walk again. Your destination is waiting for you."

- "Everything we do comes from our heart (Proverbs 4:23). Your mouth speaks what's in your heart. What fills your heart?"

- "Don't miss your "DO" season because you've placed limitations on your possibilities."

- "You've tried the alternatives, now it's time to get your S.W.A.G. back!"

Companion Products

Learn more about the additional S.W.A.G. products:

S.W.A.G. Journal

S.W.A.G. Apparel

S.W.A.G. Gift Items

S.W.A.G. Session Leader Guide

Gem Makers™
Publishing

We would love to hear about your soul-freeing journey and your triumphs on the road to getting your S.W.A.G. back! Your story just might set someone else free.

To share your story, provide feedback or to book DeYonne Parker for your next event, please:

Call: (404) 477-GEMS (4367)

Visit: www.deyonneparker.com

Email: info@deyonneparker.com

Facebook: DeyonneParker

Twitter: @DeYonneParker

About the Author

DeYonne Parker, author, speaker, coach, facilitator and performance consultant, has spent over 18 years of her life motivating, developing and coaching adults to reach their fullest potential. The combination of her corporate learning background, passion for inspiring others and her own personal testimony, is what makes Parker a stimulating speaker and powerful presenter.

Parker, the Vice President of Gem Makers, LLC., utilizes her gifts and talents to empower and encourage women and girls around the world.

When not motivating, mentoring or molding the masses, Parker is passionately carrying out the duties of her first and most loved ministry, wife and mother. She and her husband, Will, have two boys and live in Georgia. They have been known to possess master board game playing skills and will challenge anyone that steps foot in the Parker household to a rigorous game of Monopoly.

Made in the USA
Columbia, SC
22 February 2020